MW00936375

10 MINUTE LEADERSHIP

8 MINUTE LEADERSHIP

10 MINUTE LEADERSHIP

RAW*REAL*RELATABLE

HEATH ELLENBERGER

XULON PRESS

Xulon Press
2301 Lucien Way #415
Maitland, FL 32751
407.339.4217
www.xulonpress.com

© 2021 by Heath Ellenberger

All rights reserved solely by the author. The author guarantees all
contents are original and do not infringe upon the legal rights of any
other person or work. No part of this book may be reproduced in any
form without the permission of the author. The views expressed in this
book are not necessarily those of the publisher.

Paperback ISBN-13: 978-1-6628-1048-0

Ebook ISBN-13: 978-1-6628-1049-7

Dedication

I want to thank my Savior, the Lord, who set the ultimate example of leadership. He also has provided me with every opportunity I have had in life. I want to live out the purpose I believe He put on my life to serve others.

I thank my wife for the unlimited amount of support over the years; without her, my success would be minimal. There is absolutely no one else I would want by my side all those years. She is my bride, business partner, best friend, the discerner of my crazy ideas, and most importantly the love of my life.

I want to thank my parents for setting godly examples for us as we were growing up.

I'd like to thank everyone who has played major roles over the years as positive and impactful role models. There are too many to mention and I know I would forget a lot of you.

Lastly, I wish to thank you, the reader. Thank you for investing in yourself and your team.

"Please visit
www.10minuteleader.com
for a special message from Heath before diving in!"

Table of Contents

Introduction

Leadership is tough.

I don't care what type of leadership position you are in. It doesn't even have to be related to the world of work. I'm talking to all people, leading people, parents, coaches, teachers, and sports team captains.

What all those individuals have in common is that there are people who are looking to them for guidance. Whether you feel the burden of leadership on a daily basis or not, the weight of that responsibility is heavy. Also, you should honor and take the title of *the leader* of people seriously, and work consistently to improve yourself and your people.

How do you keep improving? In this fast-paced world of work that never seems to end, leadership jobs are no longer 9-5, Monday through Friday. Thanks to email, texting, and group messaging apps, you are always connected. Stressed out much? Of course, you are!

Look, there are a ton of amazing resources. For example, I have read every one of Jon Gordon's books, listened to Craig Groeschel's leadership podcasts, Patrick Lencioni's podcasts and books, and, lastly, you can't talk about leadership without mentioning John Maxwell. I am sure you have your favorites too.

The common problem with all the above personalities is they all fight for one precocious currency you don't get back, *time!* I know that I have spent many hours reading and listening over the years. Every time, I was completely satisfied with the outcome I had taken away. Invariably, I wished I could have gotten to those nuggets quicker.

This book is designed to deliver fifty-two weekly leadership lessons my team has received from me over the years. Each week, you will be served different leadership stories and lessons like my team, via email. You will be challenged to think, perform, and repeat the principles you learned.

These are raw, real, and relatable emails that contain a lot of love and emotion.

These emails will help you see and experience leadership lessons through our trials and triumphs. You will gain insight and practical application—weekly—to overcome obstacles you or your team may be facing. Leadership dilemmas can be a drag. But now, armed with an on-the-go guide, you can gain the proper position for ongoing leadership success.

Leadership is a journey, and we are always learning new ways to lead others. Join my team and me as we bring our personal and intimate weekly conversations to you.

They Deserve Better

One Sunday night in 2018, it was about seven pm. I was sitting in my office, preparing for my next week of travel. A lot of regional managers and others who travel for work can relate to those Sunday nights.

Sunday was always a day I'd review the previous week and preview the coming week. You may wonder why I was working on a Sunday. Beside the fact that I have a problem, I believe leadership never sleeps; and when you are not looking to improve your team, you should be looking to improve yourself.

As I revisited my pressure points in my current role, one common theme kept creeping into my mind: "They deserve better!"

Your team does deserve better! Have you ever heard that before? Instead of someone telling me this in a performance review, it was a voice in the back of my head expressing the thought. You know that voice that always creeps in? It's the voice that so many of us like to disregard and try to believe doesn't exist. My inner critic was talking once again, and he only seemed to get louder the longer I tried to ignore him.

It may be part of my competitive nature that I am always looking for more and better; it could also be my ADHD! The fact is that I have a hundred browser tabs open in my head—at any given moment.

Whatever the case, I wasn't satisfied with the amount of attention and consistent engagement I was having with the region. I knew that I wasn't having the impact I was hoping for them.

They referred to the managers and head coaches in the region I was supporting. At the time, I was two years in, working for one of the fastest-growing fitness franchises in the world. I was the regional sales operations and regional fitness manager for Orangetheory Fitness. At the time, my market was thirty-five studios strong with more opening.

There was always an uphill battle. We needed a consistent engagement piece that would encourage self-growth for the managers and head coaches in the studios. In our world, fast pace is an understatement. So, asking them to read or do anything outside of their normal 8-12 hour day was never going to happen.

As I sat in my office, I started to think back to my past life. I had been into fitness for over eighteen years. Like most people who start out in fitness, I started personal training at age eighteen. I have been very blessed to work with hundreds of amazing clients and members, many of whom helped shape me as much as I helped reshape them. As I was thinking back to the conversations and interactions with those clients and members, that inner critic's voice began to quiet down, and three letters kept repeating in my mind: CPR, CPR, CPR! No, I wasn't having a heart attack. It was how I kept those clients and members consistently engaged.

I started to see more clearly the correlation between exercise and leadership. Trainers lead people too. I had been so caught up in the whirlwind of the corporate business world that I'd forgotten my roots. I realized I could use the same tactics that helped build better bodies to construct better leaders.

Leadership, like exercise, requires challenges. Without challenging your body with new exercises or different weight selections, you will never create change. This was how I was able to help many clients, by consistently providing an appropriate level of challenge—every workout. This was the first piece of the puzzle I was trying to solve; they needed a weekly challenging thought and exercise.

The next relationship that leadership and exercising have in common is *you have to perform, the simple act of taking action*. To perform, you have to have a relatable starting point. For example, if I wanted to have a client perform a new exercise, I would have to show and explain the movement. So, I would perform the action first, then allow my clients to perform. It was then my job to correct along the way. What I needed was a relatable starting point to help them understand how to perform better.

One more! You ever hear that from your trainer or coach? They are referring to that last final effort. That final rep, the one that's going to force change. Repetitions are what ties it all together. Once you have the challenge, then you understand how to perform it correctly. Now it's all about getting your reps in. Different types of goals require different reps ranges in the world of weightlifting. However, the common theme is *repeat efforts consistently*. As a leader, you must get your reps in with your leadership muscles.

Now that I had a foundation of CPR (I am a huge acronym guy, you will learn), I started to draft an email. Little did I know the effect that email would have, and that I would still be writing them almost three years later.

Just One Email

I am no longer with the corporate office of Orangetheory Fitness. I am now the operating partner and franchisee of nine studios. My wife and I are so blessed that God delivered our business partners to us. Our partners are passionate, God-loving, and people-loving individuals, which aligns with our beliefs as well.

As I am writing this, it's 2021. You immediately think about all the turmoil the world of work and people are experiencing currently, which is why I feel God was directing me toward writing this book.

During the shutdown last year, our businesses were closed, and my wife and I needed a break from everything. So, we went on a long walk together and just talked like we hadn't talked in years. We were asking all the *what-if* questions that many are still asking today. Then like I do many times (again, I'll blame it on my ADHD), I told her I was going to write a book. Startled but not surprised, that comment came out of left field. But after ten years, she is used to my quirkiness.

Upon returning home, I grabbed my computer and started writing. After about a month, I had developed a pretty good storyline, and the characters were coming to life. Then our businesses were allowed to re-open.

I got pulled in no less than a hundred different directions every day. I hate to say it, but my book become the last priority. I was more worried about making sure our teams had support, and we were going to be able to be flexible and adapt to the new, ever-changing business environment.

There remained one consistency from before: those Sunday emails to my team. I felt as they were more important than ever now. The group receiving the emails was smaller now; they went out to just our managers and assistant managers. But the emails began to transform. They had new life, new challenges, we were all facing together. The emails were becoming a leadership MapQuest for our managers.

When I first started to write the emails, it was a way for me to consistently engage with every person in leadership within the studio in the region. The emails helped to address problems the region may have been experiencing. It provided that weekly touch point and moments of positive impact I knew every leader needs.

The success came in the form of *thank-you* text messages, phone calls, and emails. These managers and head coaches were able to start developing leadership soft skills on a regular basis. They would call me when they applied one of the topics discussed and tell me about their success with a stubborn staff member. Or, they might have seen a breakthrough they'd had in an area of their business that was struggling. This was the success I had always hoped for when I was training clients, small weekly wins. Sometimes it was showing up to all three workouts that week. Other times, it was hitting a personal best on their mile. Whatever the success, I was living out my motive of *impacting people in a positive way.*

I looked back at the success of these small, weekly nuggets and the impact they were having with our team. I was able to finally see what God was using those emails for all along. When I first began writing these emails, it was only to have a positive impact on those who were in the region. These emails were the book I was *supposed* to be writing. I started to think, what if I could serve others our weekly leadership lessons and stories? How many more people could we positively impact?

What do those in leadership roles want and need to succeed, it's learning from experiences others have had and how they overcame them. Then, they must be able to apply it to their situations.

Even though we are in the fitness industry, we aren't much different than other businesses. Outside of loud music, heavy breathing, and sweating. However, we still had sales numbers we had to hit. We have marketing that needs to be done. We have staff we have to lead, teach, and correct. We have members who we need to serve.

These emails were addressed toward a fitness audience. Covering all the main issues above, I could have changed them for you and made them more "business generic," but I wanted them to be as authentic as possible. So, where you see *member,* replace it with *customer.* When you see the word *coach,* replace it with the title of the people who provide your customers with an experience. We call our businesses *studios.* Replace that with whatever you call your business.

If you are new to leadership, or maybe your leadership needs a little CPR right now, I can promise you if you spend ten minutes every Sunday reading one of these emails, you will hopefully be entertained but, more importantly, challenged. Be encouraged to perform the tasks and exercises. Lastly, the piece that is on you is to repeat this process weekly. Like when trying to get bigger biceps or lose a few pounds, you can't do it in a week. But if you stay dedicated and focus on your CPR report every week, you will begin to see results.

Leaders, this is a call to break out of the mediocrity of your routine. It will only take ten minutes of your time. Why? Because, "They Deserve Better!"

Ugh, it's that time of year. It's especially felt in the fitness industry—resolution time. You know what I say to that this year… go kick rocks resolutions. The year 2020 taught us how easily your resolution can be stripped away. Did your resolutions make it to mid-March? We know that 80 percent of people don't make it past February. Your plans were ripped out from underneath you, and there was nothing you could do about it.

I know for a fact this year there are going to be people who are like me. I want to have full control: control over my decisions, destination, and destiny.

Are you like me?

I am going to ask you to join me on a forty-five-day leadership challenge.

If you are interested, keep reading. Are you like me? Nah, you say. I want to do things how I have always done them. Well, that's okay too: I can't drive you to get better, challenge yourself, or to blow past obstacles. But, it's totally okay if you aren't in a season to be challenged, and 2020 was challenging enough. Then I would ask that you encourage those in this group who are going to step out and challenge themselves over the next forty-five days.

If you are still reading, I am going to assume two things— you are ready to suit up and go to battle with me, or you are reading to see what the others are getting themselves into. So for the second group, at this point, there is no way you're interested. You have already made up your mind. If you don't have butterflies in your stomach and a little anxiousness, then you aren't suiting up.

For those of you who are lacing up your boots, this is the part of the email you have been waiting for. This is where you will find your fate for the next forty-five days.

The goal of this forty-five-day leadership challenge is to encourage you out of your current leadership rut by testing your mental, emotional, and physical stamina. By the end of the forty-five days, you will emerge with a new perspective about yourself. You will have better self-control, work capacity, leadership capabilities, and healthier body composition: all while being motivated by a collective of leaders surrounding you.

Forty-Five Day Leadership Challenge Rules:

Mental Challenges:

Pick one leadership/business book and read for a minimum of twenty minutes or ten pages, whichever comes first.

- Keep a journal with one takeaway per day.
- If you would like book recommendations, I have a ton.
- I would encourage you to pick a subject that you feel you need extra guidance on.

Listen to one leadership/business/sales podcast each week.

- Keep a journal of three to four key takeaways.

Choose a minimum of one bullet point below for the next 45 days:

- Eliminate alcohol

- Reduce alcohol to one drink per week

- Eliminate cheat meals (I don't want to tell you a specific diet routine to follow. I do want to encourage you to remove some guilty food pleasures. This could be anything processed, high in sugar, trans fats, the list could go on. This is your challenge; make it something you can live with and achieve.)

- Reduce cheat meals to one meal per week

- Eliminate soda

- Reduce soda to one per week

Ask one person per week for personal feedback (three areas of feedback below to ask for). Then, journal it for later use.

- How can you lead that person better?

- How can you improve your leadership?

- How can you support them?

Emotional Challenges:

Take a team member out for coffee once a week.

- Write in your journal about something you learned and how that can help you become a better leader.

- This doesn't have to be someone who works directly under you. That would be a good place to start though.

Do something nice for your team once per week.

- Journal what it was and what responses or results it gave.

Get involved with one charity event.

- If you do more, great.

Physical Challenges:

Work out a minimum of forty-five minutes every day.

- This could include:
- OTF
- Outdoor run
- Walking the dogs on a recovery day
- Weight training
- Yoga
- Anything that is going to get your body moving and HR elevated for forty-five minutes

Drink a minimum of 64 oz of water each day.

Set two workout goals you want to achieve each week.

- Write these goals down in your journal and circle them when you achieve the goal.
- Examples:
- Burn "X" number of calories for the week
- Earn "X" number of splat points per class
- Increase your speed or weights

At the end of the forty-five days, we will have a leadership get-together; and this is where all the grit over the last forty-five days will come into play. More on this to come.

Who's ready to join me?

Subject: **CPR Report**

Free Space to write down key takeaways or answers to any questions found in this week's email:

_____

_____

_____

_____

Questions

Answer any challenging questions the email posed to you:

_____

_____

_____

Challenge

What was the leadership challenge that spoke to you this week?

_____

_____

_____

_____

Perform

How do you plan to perform the challenges this week?

_____

_____

_____

_____

Repetitions

What do you need to do to remind yourself to get your reps in this week?

_____

_____

_____

_____

CPR Progress Report

(1 Needed Major Improvement - 5 CRUSHED IT!)

Rate yourself 1-5 on your leadership challenge this week

1   2   3   4   5

Rate 1-5 how well do you think you performed this week

1   2   3   4   5

Rate 1-5 how often you feel like you were consistent with your reps this week

1   2   3   4   5

Subject: Vision

I don't paint. Honestly, I was never a very good art student. I guess I was not gifted with an artistic hand.

Picture with me an artist getting ready to paint a picture.

First, I'm sure you have to pick out the right-sized canvas. Not all works of art come on an 8x10.

Faith and I were walking around downtown last night and walked into a gallery. There was a beautiful painting on a surfboard. So I can imagine this is a very important step. You must choose the proper backdrop to display your art.

Once you have the perfect canvas that is going to capture your masterpiece, you have to gather the appropriate tools. Not all paintbrushes are created equal. I'm not even going to go into all the different types because, honestly, I have no idea. I do know if you are trying to paint small details, you aren't going to have a large, bushy brush.

Lastly, you have the colors. These are what will breathe life into your masterpiece. The correct colors will stop and demand the attention of those admiring the piece.

So now you have everything you need to get started, right?

WRONG!

You forgot your vision! You can have all the best canvas, brushes, and colors. But if you step to a blank canvas without a vision, you're not only going to waste a lot of time, but you'll end up never really getting started.

You don't have to comprehend the full vision in your head, but maybe just a word; just one word that can give your art purpose. You don't have to have all the answers or even know the exact colors you are going to use. But if you step to your canvas with one word, it will inspire you for the rest. Can you start to see your picture come into the frame?

I had challenged you all to come up with one word for your studios this year. I also challenged you to personally come up with one word for the year 2021.

I am excited to hear everyone's word tomorrow on our call.

I wanted to take a quick second and share mine with you.

I did mine a little differently this year. I looked at mine like a painting, and I dissected my word into a few different parts. This helped me to really define my word and give it some weight. I needed a heavy word this year.

My word is COACH.

Wow, Heath, super creative word. We use that word every day in our work lives.

Yes, this is true, which is why I stripped it apart and I gave each letter some weight and responsibility. I will not be defined by just the word COACH, but what each letter represents.

I thought about coaches I have had in the past; coaches I know and coaches I have watched and read about. I thought about my own coaching over the last almost nineteen years.

I don't want to look at this as just an acronym, but a word that carries multiple purposes.

Over the next four weeks, I want to share with you what each letter represents and the burden I have placed on myself to represent each letter as it is defined.

I'll start with the first letter.

C—Courage: That word in itself almost made me want to stop this experiment. That's a weighty word! Courage is what every great coach I have ever known, watched, or read about has. We, as people, are called to be courageous. People want a courageous coach. Think about those workouts or practices that are so tough you feel like you might die. No one wants a wimpy coach at those moments. You want a courageous coach by your side, one you know you can lean on when you feel like you don't have anything left in the tank. There are times for hugs but not now; it's time for hustle.

When uncertainty rattles the state of your team or business, you need a courageous coach to lean on when you feel like it's all falling apart. You need that courageous coach when the hurt of the season's final loss feels like it will never go away. You need a courageous coach to tell you it's temporary and that we learned for next year.

After a year that has produced so much fear, it only felt right to start with courage.

So team commitment number one from me to you:

I will be there to lean on when you need support.

Have you really thought about your word? Did you give life to your word, or did you just pick one because you had to?

Team 2021 isn't about fear; it's about courage! You'll need courage to stay in the game, even when the score makes it look impossible.

bject: CPR Report

Free Space to write down key takeaways or answers to any questions found in this week's email:

_____

_____

_____

_____

Questions

Answer any challenging questions the email posed to you:

_____

_____

_____

_____

Challenge

What was the leadership challenge that spoke to you this week?

_____

_____

_____

_____

Perform

How do you plan to perform the challenges this week?

_____

_____

_____

_____

Repetitions

What do you need to do to remind yourself to get your reps in this week?

_____

_____

_____

_____

CPR Progress Report

(1 Needed Major Improvement - 5 CRUSHED IT!)

Rate yourself 1-5 on your leadership challenge this week

1   2   3   4   5

Rate 1-5 how well do you think you performed this week

1   2   3   4   5

Rate 1-5 how often you feel like you were consistent with your reps this week

1   2   3   4   5

You know what I love about football? The hard hits; acrobatic catches; the last-minute, nail-biting field goal attempts? Well, yes, all of those!

But something I enjoy even more is watching the coaches. Every coach has a different approach to his players, the game, the other coaches, the refs.

Which brings us to the second letter in my word, which is O.

This stands for OBSERVE. You can learn so much when you just take a moment to observe your surroundings and other people.

I have learned so much over the years from observing other coaches. When I was a younger trainer coming up the ranks, I was always learning and observing.

As a matter of fact, I would also take the approach of being observed. There were a lot of guys I looked up to in the industry. I'd approach a class I was coaching like they were there observing me. Why? Because it elevated my approach as a coach.

If you aren't observing other leaders and coaches out there, you are missing out. There is a lot to be learned by merely observing.

I want to give you three F words to observe when looking at your team.

The first is I want you to observe their *focus*.

If you are a football coach, you don't have to ask most players if they are ready to play; you can just look into their eyes. There will be an intensity and passion in their eyes before a game.

In the same setting, you can also observe a lack of focus. If you are giving a pregame speech, and they are looking around the room or talking to another player, that's a definite lack of focus.

When coaching members, you can tell who is there to set a 2000-meter row PR and who is there because they want to burn some calories. Either way, it's okay. You, as a coach, just have to observe their level of focus and coach toward that.

Now when it comes to your team, they aren't walking into work with an *eye of the tiger* type focus to make a sale. If they are, never let them leave!

However, you can observe very quickly who is excited to be there and going to put in a solid day's work and who is there to punch the clock.

Use this observation to coach them based on their focus.

Those who want to punch the clock may need a little more nudging. Constantly nudging your team can be exhausting on the coach's part. Make sure you don't let mediocre focus hang around too long without addressing it.

The ones who are focused will see the mediocrity and will quickly fall victim to it.

Like any team, if you are putting in 100 percent effort every day, but everyone else is giving 70 percent, over time, you will end up giving 70 percent with them. Because no more is being required, no more will be given.

If everyone's eyes are glazed over, you knew that energy high is absent.

Next, as a coach, I want to observe their *form*. There will always be those who need a little more correcting than others. These are the ones who haven't had as many reps to let their bodies adapt to the movement. So these are your new team members. They just need you to coach them long enough to get the proper reps in.

The second type of form correction is the ones who have been doing it wrong for a long time and you have to break that improper movement pattern. These are tough; their bodies want to fight you because it's more comfortable doing it the way they have always done it, even though it's wrong. Take your time and correct in layers. First, start with major issues, and then work your way to the smaller details. Don't try to do it all at once.

The third type isn't a correction but a praise. When someone is crushing it and their form is spot on, let them know. Make them feel like a million dollars. I promise you not only will they work harder for you, but they will take it to the next level.

The last F I want to observe as a coach is *fatigue*. Know when enough pushing is enough; or, know where to push a little more.

Signs of fatigue are different for everyone, but there is one common theme of fatigue—lack of interest. Really? Yes. When you become fatigued with anything, you will develop a lack of interest. There are many factors that contribute to a lack of interest.

You have to find ways to avoid the lack of interest from setting in. For most of your team, this is just a job for them, which can quickly lead to a lack of interest. So if you begin to push too hard, like those who really don't like exercising, they will get turned off and lose interest.

You have to know when and where to push, but, more importantly, know when to back off. If you begin to push past fatigue, not only will you lose the respect of your team, you will lose any momentum you've gained with them. They are too exhausted to keep up their drive. There will always be another day to push, so don't push your team to fatigue.

This week, I would like you to observe the three Fs with your team.

Make some notes on what you observed. I will be interested to hear about them.

bject: CPR Report

Free Space to write down key takeaways or answers to any questions found in this week's email:

_____

_____

_____

_____

Questions

Answer any challenging questions the email posed to you:

_____

_____

_____

_____

Challenge

What was the leadership challenge that spoke to you this week?

_____

_____

_____

_____

Perform

How do you plan to perform the challenges this week?

_____

_____

_____

_____

Repetitions

What do you need to do to remind yourself to get your reps in this week?

_____

_____

_____

_____

CPR Progress Report

(1 Needed Major Improvement - 5 CRUSHED IT!)

Rate yourself 1-5 on your leadership challenge this week

1   2   3   4   5

Rate 1-5 how well do you think you performed this week

1   2   3   4   5

Rate 1-5 how often you feel like you were consistent with your reps this week

1   2   3   4   5

WRONG!

When I was thinking of an "A" word for my acronym, it came to me as I was watching a football game. See a common theme here; it's all about coaching!

What do players do after they leave the field? They immediately go grab a Microsoft surface and begin to *analyze* the previous plays. They don't just go back out on the field and sling the ball around. They take time to analyze the formation of the defense and other possible windows of opportunity they might take advantage of.

Great coaches are always looking for an advantage when it comes to analyzing.

What I want to focus on is analyzing your time and your

presence.

Let's unpack what it means to analyze your time. As you all know, I identified that time management was a major topic for 2021, after some observations I made this past year.

Where does time management start? With an analysis of your time spent and impact of outcome, it's a pretty basic formula:

If I spend x time doing y, how great is the z outcome?

Let me share a quick personal example with you.

I create and post the content for all nine studios' social media pages every week. So let's say it's about two hours to create content and another hour to post it all. What's the return on that time investment for me or the businesses? It's not very high. We don't really generate any revenue from those posts; our team doesn't learn anything or get better from those posts. But they are necessary in the world of business social media.

What do you do every week that sucks up time but doesn't create revenue, positive studio growth, or staff improvement?

That's the first key to time management. I want you to take some time this week and see how long it takes you to do certain tasks. Then analyze time spent and overall outcome.

Could you have been doing something of higher value with your time at that moment?

Along with analyzing your time, I want to now think about your presence. Analyze where you are best when.

For example, if you have a weak closing percentage, your presence is needed when you have fresh opportunities in the studio. You can't fix a problem if you aren't there to observe it.

I want you to analyze your presence. Think about a starting QB: Do they play in the last game of the year if they already locked down a playoff spot? Usually, NO! Why? Because if they get hurt, the consequences are much greater than losing a game that doesn't matter.

As coaches/leaders, we want to make more strategic decisions by analyzing our time and our presence.

Analyze three things this week that suck away your valuable time.

Analyze where your presence is needed in your business this week moving forward.

Subject: CPR Report

Free Space to write down key takeaways or answers to any questions found in this week's email:

_____

_____

_____

_____

Questions

Answer any challenging questions the email posed to you:

_____

_____

_____

_____

Challenge

What was the leadership challenge that spoke to you this week?

_____

_____

_____

_____

Perform

How do you plan to perform the challenges this week?

_____

_____

_____

_____

Repetitions

What do you need to do to remind yourself to get your reps in this week?

_____

_____

_____

_____

CPR Progress Report

(1 Needed Major Improvement - 5 CRUSHED IT!)

Rate yourself 1-5 on your leadership challenge this week

1   2   3   4   5

Rate 1-5 how well do you think you performed this week

1   2   3   4   5

Rate 1-5 how often you feel like you were consistent with your reps this week

1   2   3   4   5

Subject: You're a Genius!

When you hear the word *genius,* you probably think of people like Albert Einstein or Thomas Jefferson. Do you really ever think of yourself as being a genius? I know I don't. I was a terrible student growing up.

There were always things I was good at; it just never seemed to apply to school. I have always had an entrepreneurial spirit; that doesn't really help with passing geometry class. Therefore, school, for me, ended up being a lot of social time, which I found out I was fantastic at too. You know what I was never good at? Totally completing projects. I just thought all along it was my ADHD because that's what my "disability" was. So why not blame it on that? It seemed logical and well; I needed to blame it on something.

You are thinking, Heath, *coach* does not have the letter G in it. I know, I told you I was a bad student, but I can spell coach. The next letter is C, and I want to create a *culture* of geniuses.

Don't worry; that doesn't mean I am looking to hire an entirely new staff. I would be the first one to go, if that was the case.

If you can think back to May of 2020, when we opened up after the COVID shutdown. We sat in the conference room and all took the opportunity to introduce ourselves and what we did for the region. A lot of you were confused because you didn't have a clearly defined title. Do you remember what I told you?

I told you that I don't like titles because I feel they are restrictive. I felt like using the word *title* too many times prevents us from helping in areas we may actually be able to add a ton of value to. But if our title doesn't say we do that, then we shouldn't.

But I gave you all titles anyway because that's how business works, right? Listen, business used to work a lot differently before March 2020. Business has changed a lot.

If you asked me, instead of having a region full of directors and managers who are restricted to a department or studio, I would love to have a region full of geniuses. These geniuses have amazing, God-given abilities to contribute to the region. That's exactly what we have, thanks to the working genius assessment we all took a few months back.

You all know I am a huge fan of this concept. I guess it's because I can see how it has applied to my life as far back as I can remember. Remember how I told you I would just blame not finishing projects on my ADHD? I don't have that excuse now; I know that tenacity is a working frustration of mine. Knowing that I can either have a better game plan to finish projects, or I can lean on one of our geniuses who are *tenacity people*, God knew what He was doing when He brought faith into my life.

After having this working genius assessment now for a few months, here is how I would love to continue building a culture of geniuses.

First, I have really enjoyed working with the other I (Invention) geniuses in the region; there are three of us. It's great knowing that I don't always have to be the idea guy. Don't get me wrong; I have always been that guy. Quick story—I was in fifth grade and I ran for class president. I ran on the platform of getting new playground equipment. No joke. Guess what? I won. I helped create a fundraiser for new playground equipment. The sad part is that my class never saw the new equipment but the classes after us got to enjoy it.

Anyway, my point is working with our other invention geniuses takes a lot of the pressure off of me! I love the workflow of starting with the ideation group. It allows us the freedom of exploring ideas and concepts without the activation people stopping us before we get all the way through an idea. I have seen a great deal of success working inside of our geniuses.

I would like to set up a *board of geniuses*. This board would tackle initiatives and issues. We will have each of the stages represented: Ideation (W, I) Activation (D, G) Implementation (E, T). This will allow for blending workflow through each of the stages while avoiding your working frustrations. I believe blending our geniuses together will allow us to not only be more efficient in rolling out initiatives, but we will be more effective at solving issues.

Secondly, this is for you, team. Wouldn't it be nice to have your staff know your genius? I do. I think your team would appreciate knowing what your working frustrations are. Wait, was that a curveball? No, you have heard me say this before. Let's say, for example, you aren't a galvanizer, but your team is looking to you for encouragement and excitement. It doesn't mean you can't do it, but it drains you over time. So, you will become frustrated knowing you need to motivate your team, but just don't want to or aren't naturally good at it. They will become frustrated because they are looking for the motivation from you but not getting it. So now everyone is frustrated because of your working frustration.

Instead of that nasty cycle of frustration, it would be better to have them know what you naturally avoid. Then they can come to you for the topics you are naturally gifted at. To be honest, that may provide them with the motivation they are looking for because they are getting your best!

How have you used your genius since learning about it?

Have you found ways to integrate your genius into your daily patterns of life, not just work?

Have you found a genius partner? This is someone who has an opposite genius you need.

This year, let's create a culture of geniuses, not just titles and positions.

Subject: CPR Report

Free Space to write down key takeaways or answers to any questions found in this week's email:

_____

_____

_____

_____

Questions

Answer any challenging questions the email posed to you:

_____

_____

_____

_____

Challenge

What was the leadership challenge that spoke to you this week?

_____

_____

_____

_____

Perform

How do you plan to perform the challenges this week?

_____

_____

_____

_____

Repetitions

What do you need to do to remind yourself to get your reps in this week?

_____

_____

_____

_____

CPR Progress Report

(1 Needed Major Improvement - 5 CRUSHED IT!)

Rate yourself 1-5 on your leadership challenge this week

1   2   3   4   5

Rate 1-5 how well do you think you performed this week

1   2   3   4   5

Rate 1-5 how often you feel like you were consistent with your reps this week

1   2   3   4   5

Subject: **What the H?**

Hahahahaha! You probably thought I was going to say humble or something like that. Come on, now!

Do coaches/leaders have to be humble? Yes, of course, but there are other emails with those lessons.

Humor is the final word of COACH. Hmmm, maybe I went a little overboard on this one. But I think it's super important we talk about humor as a coach and leader.

Why? Well, I never have before and when I started to really think about my word, I dissected it to be more purposeful. I wanted to challenge myself to look deeper into all the characteristics great coaches and leaders have. Not just the billboard words; those are the ones that are thrown around all the time.

I really think humor gets overlooked. I don't know why; maybe some feel it's taboo in the workplace environment. Some feel humor can be offensive; others may think they aren't that funny.

Good news. You don't have to be a comedian to make people laugh.

I was thinking about how many laughs we all shared at our leadership meeting at the trampoline/ninja warrior/laser tag place. Guys, do you realize how much laughter was going on? Guess what? No one told a single joke. I believe we all became a little closer because we shared some good laughs.

You are probably thinking, *Well, great, now I have to take my team to play trampoline dodgeball every week.* Not the case.

You can inject humor into your everyday routine. I'll give you a quick example. When I coach class, I say some funny stuff to members that makes them laugh. It breaks the ice of intensity. Have you ever been in a situation where the tension was so intense? Then, someone said or did something that made everyone laugh. It's those moments we need to be able to have with our teams. You are like the MC of the comedy show. You don't have to have all the good jokes; leave that for the professional. But you have a couple good one-liners that you can toss in there now and then when needed.

I want to look at one way you can use humor in your day-to-day leadership.

First, I want you to think about humor like a base pace interval on an endurance day. Endurance days are all about longer efforts of the mid-range intensities. You are creating a breathless environment for yourself to live in, for anywhere between one and four minutes at a time. Just when you feel like you aren't able to maintain it any longer, your coach says, "*3,2,1 BASE PACE.*" You are thinking to yourself, *Thank you!* Even if it's only a one-minute base pace, it offers just enough relief from those mentally and physically challenging intervals.

You can't have a whole workout that consists of just base paces. You would never have progress. Your body needs those more intense efforts to create change, like your business and your team. Our business can't become a comedy show. If that was the case, we would never get anything done. Our businesses need those intense moments to grow as well. But we also need to inject some humorous moments now and then to add some stress relief for our teams.

What to do when you notice your team needs a humor base pace:

- Send the team a funny meme in a text/group message app.

- Pick someone on the team to find the funniest, "Why did the chicken cross the road?" joke (work appropriate).

- Share a personal story of a blunder you had professionally (we all have had them, it's okay to laugh at yourself).

- If it's the middle of the day and your studio is slow, play a game with your team. Things like Catchphrase or Heads Up are great quick games that will allow for some laughs.

- Have a fun/funny training session. (Just make sure they don't feel like hazing sessions.)

  - Have the team sit into an Iso squat and pick each one to give you the five major objections.

  - Cut out the words in the mission statement and play *pin the word in the spalt*. The goal is to have them fit all the mission statement words into the center of the splat.

  - You could have a power hour call contest. Split your team into two. For each phone call they make, they get to shoot a paper ball into the trash can. The team with the most scores by the end of the hour wins.

What's most important to remember is these moments are to recover your team from intense efforts. Think about the example I used when I am coaching a class. When I see someone who is fatigued, I may use humor with that person as a form of encouragement instead of "pushing" him/her to give more effort.

Humor, I believe, makes you more relatable as a leader. People love to laugh and enjoy the place in which they work. If you can have a sense of humor as a leader, it says a lot to your team. Humor, in a way, shows you are down to earth.

Has your workplace's sense of humor experienced a drought recently?

Where and when do you need to infuse some humor into your daily routine?

This week, try to have at least two moments of humor with your team. See what the outcome is from a performance standpoint.

Over time, take note of:

- Do I feel my team is building more trust in me?

- Do I see them smiling more often?

- Do they seem more excited to be at work?

Team, I hope over the last four weeks you have thought about your word for the year and given some deeper meaning to it.

Subject: CPR Report

Free Space to write down key takeaways or answers to any questions found in this week's email:

_____

_____

_____

_____

Questions

Answer any challenging questions the email posed to you:

_____

_____

_____

_____

Challenge

What was the leadership challenge that spoke to you this week?

_____

_____

_____

_____

Perform

How do you plan to perform the challenges this week?

_____

_____

_____

_____

Repetitions

What do you need to do to remind yourself to get your reps in this week?

_____

_____

_____

_____

CPR Progress Report

(1 Needed Major Improvement - 5 CRUSHED IT!)

Rate yourself 1-5 on your leadership challenge this week

1   2   3   4   5

Rate 1-5 how well do you think you performed this week

1   2   3   4   5

Rate 1-5 how often you feel like you were consistent with your reps this week

1   2   3   4   5

Subject: **P=MV**

I know what you are thinking; another one of Heath's crazy math equations. Well, kind of, but not entirely.

I wanted to get back to the weekly leadership newsletters I was writing in the past.

So, I felt why not start with talking a little about MO! Has MO visited you this month? How about this week? Or, has MO taken a little vacation?

Who the heck is MO! No, not the creepy guy in the back of the theater, sitting all alone in a Harry Potter cape!

We are talking about *Momentum*.

P= momentum

M= mass

V= velocity

Momentum is the power of an object when moving, and the force it can have on another object.

Hopefully, this was a little reminder from middle school!

So, why the heck am I talking about MO?

John Maxwell says, "Momentum can solve 80% of your problems."

Think about that statement for a second. Picture these two scenarios and see how you feel when you read both. Think about how your teammates feel. You, the home team. You are down two touchdowns going into the fourth quarter.

You have the ball in the red zone. Third down and your QB tosses an interception.

How do you feel?

How does the defense taking the field feel?

What happened to the stadium? (This goes back to when fans were allowed.)

Now picture this.

You are the home team. Down two touchdowns going into the fourth quarter. The opposing team is in the red zone, about to go up three scores. When the play begins, the QB gets rushed and is forced to pitch the ball to the running back. As the running rounds the end, the ball is stripped from behind. The linebacker picks up the ball and starts to run toward your end zone. He's finally brought down after a sixty-yard swing.

How do you feel?

How does the offense feel taking the field?

What happened to the stadium?

Now the key isn't riding the high of the fumble. That is a short-lived momentum; as quickly as it was gained, it can as easily disappear.

The key is to use the momentum to shift the mindset of the players. To utilize the small wins will compound that momentum. Every yard gained is a momentum shift.

I'm not talking about momentum because it's football season. I'm taking about momentum because we have it right now. I want to encourage you to KEEP it. The minute your team feels momentum shifting, there is a small depression that sets in. Excitement starts to deflate, productivity dwindles, and culture deteriorates. Those 4Ds can stop a moving train.

See? Once you lose the momentum, it takes time, resources, and a ton of energy to get it back.

I want to encourage you all with three ways to keep your momentum up and throw some more coal in that engine:

- Celebrate the small wins with your team. I know we don't always get a chance to do this because we are busy. Find the time. Make the effort. Be genuine.

- Don't let your team see you slip up. The coach can throw momentum as easily as the players. The players have to trust their coach's ability to not just *keep* momentum, but increase it. Is there an area where you might be slipping? Are there phone calls coming in that your SAs are taking from members who said you're slipping? Be proactive and remember, just because it's urgent, it's not always important. Do me a favor: Write down the top five things you have to do tomorrow when you get in. Then cross off the three that can wait. We will talk about this on the call at 12:30.

- Momentum is all about the future, not the past. The past never gets anyone excited. It already happened; that excitement is already gone. Just because you made a sale yesterday doesn't get you geeked to make another one today. Find ways to forecast momentum for your team and get them excited about tomorrow, today.

Let's have an amazing week, everyone.

bject: CPR Report

Free Space to write down key takeaways or answers to any
questions found in this week's email:

_____

_____

_____

_____

Questions

Answer any challenging questions the email posed to you:

_____

_____

_____

_____

Challenge

What was the leadership challenge that spoke to you
this week?

_____

_____

_____

_____

Perform

How do you plan to perform the challenges this week?

_____

_____

_____

_____

Repetitions

What do you need to do to remind yourself to get your reps in this week?

_____

_____

_____

_____

CPR Progress Report

(1 Needed Major Improvement - 5 CRUSHED IT!)

Rate yourself 1-5 on your leadership challenge this week

1   2   3   4   5

Rate 1-5 how well do you think you performed this week

1   2   3   4   5

Rate 1-5 how often you feel like you were consistent with your reps this week

1   2   3   4   5

bject: Are You Hot?

No, that's not an HR question; it's another acronym. So take a second and calm down. Leadership is tough, not to mention when you are looking at yourself as a leader through others' perspectives. It's one thing to see yourself as a leader; it's a whole other thing to see what others see you as a leader.

Which is where this email is going to take us this evening.

This is challenge week as a leader of our studios. I am challenging you to be:

- Humble
- Open
- Transparent

How can you be a leader and also be humble? Shouldn't I be strong and display my power so everyone knows I am the boss? Aren't my ways of doing things better than others? If I am humble, doesn't that make me a weak leader?

I can assure you if you are thinking any of the above, then this is going to be a tough week for you.

Humility is so far from being weak. I actually believe humility is at the core of any great leader.

The Humility Challenge of the week:

- Ask how you can help your employees do their jobs... then LISTEN!

- Create a safe space for employees where they don't feel intimidated(I would suggest a coffee shop or really anywhere outside of an office)...then LISTEN!

- Seek input from other leaders about their observations of you as a leader...then LISTEN!

Caution... Only do the above if you truly intend to change. So listen with an open mind and a humble heart.

Now, on to the next; this one is pretty simple but can be painful. Painful? Yes, it's hard to open up and receive real, true feedback in a constructive environment. But this one is going to be simple.

Open up the challenge of the week:

- Take ten minutes and talk with your team and ask for a pulse check review. It's really simple; these are the two questions.

  o What are two things you value from my leadership?

  o What are two areas you would like me to improve?

Okay, take a second, stand up, and shake that one out. Might want to get some extra kombucha on that day to help settle your stomach.

Transparency is like humility; it's a key characteristic of leadership. Transparency closes the leadership trust triangle with humility and openness.

Transparency Challenge for the week:

- Share your vision for the team this month ... Show 'em the WHY.

- Share your team's performance last month ... Offer praise and WINS.

- Discuss solutions for pressure points ...
  Explain the WHY.

As we continue on the journey of becoming the leader that others crave, we will be a little acidic before we are craved. These exercises will help cut the acidity of your leadership.

Subject: CPR Report

Free Space to write down key takeaways or answers to any questions found in this week's email:

_____

_____

_____

_____

Questions

Answer any challenging questions the email posed to you:

_____

_____

_____

_____

Challenge

What was the leadership challenge that spoke to you this week?

_____

_____

_____

_____

Perform

How do you plan to perform the challenges this week?

_____

_____

_____

_____

Repetitions

What do you need to do to remind yourself to get your reps in this week?

_____

_____

_____

_____

CPR Progress Report

(1 Needed Major Improvement - 5 CRUSHED IT!)

Rate yourself 1-5 on your leadership challenge this week

1   2   3   4   5

Rate 1-5 how well do you think you performed this week

1   2   3   4   5

Rate 1-5 how often you feel like you were consistent with your reps this week

1   2   3   4   5

Subject: What's Your Perspective of Success?

I had the privilege of being on a podcast recently for the Orangetheory Network. I was asked this question along with others, but this one specifically was hard to digest at first. As I'm writing this, its 2020 and we are currently in a global pandemic. Politics aside, whatever you believe is what you believe. That has nothing to do with the fact that this has change the world of work in the year 2020; not only work but, more importantly, mindset.

If you'd asked me, at the end of December last year, what success looked like, I would have shown you my twenty-plus page, 2020 business/sales playbook.

Do you have a good grip on perspective? I guess that's a great place to start. I read a book by Andy Andrews called "The Noticer." I'll never forget the scene about perspective. There is a wiser, old man talking with a younger, homeless man trying to find his way. They meet up on a beach to have dinner. The older man brings a can of Vienna sausage and sardines.

The old man asked, "What are you eating and where are you eating it?"

The young man answered, very practically, "Sardines and Vienna sausage, in the sand."

The old man responded with, "You ate sardines and Vienna sausage in the sand? I had surf and turf with an ocean view."

It's funny how quickly your perspective can change, based on your current situation.

When the shutdowns happened, I watched people, a lot of them. I watched how quickly their previous perspectives changed.

Your perspective of success will crumble when you place your value of success in a single viewpoint. If your view of success was how much money you were making, well then, yes, you were probably very disappointed. If you placed success in your position and were furloughed, you were devastated. If you placed success in anything outside of your control, you were discouraged.

How do you avoid damage to your view of success? I can only speak for myself and how I was able to quickly shift my mindset. I think all leaders can use this one tactic not just during a pandemic, but on a daily basis to refocus themselves.

Wake up with a purpose.

I noticed a lot of people felt helpless during the time of the lockdown. That's because for a lot of people, work is their identity and without it, they lack purpose. You are so much more than your title or position. I know it's tough to sit around and do nothing. That doesn't mean you have to lose your purpose. With purpose, you will always find someone or something to impact.

If you or your team starting to lose purpose, help gain it back by asking them a few critical questions:

- What do you love about your work?

- How do you want to be remembered?

- Why do you work?

- Do you find that your work is worthwhile?

- If so, why?

- If not, why?

Don't lose the perspective of purpose. Your team and so many depend on *you*. Your purpose is to lead.

ubject: CPR Report

Free Space to write down key takeaways or answers to any questions found in this week's email:

_____

_____

_____

_____

Questions

Answer any challenging questions the email posed to you:

_____

_____

_____

_____

Challenge

What was the leadership challenge that spoke to you this week?

_____

_____

_____

_____

Perform

How do you plan to perform the challenges this week?

_____

_____

_____

_____

Repetitions

What do you need to do to remind yourself to get your reps in this week?

_____

_____

_____

_____

CPR Progress Report

(1 Needed Major Improvement - 5 CRUSHED IT!)

Rate yourself 1-5 on your leadership challenge this week

1   2   3   4   5

Rate 1-5 how well do you think you performed this week

1   2   3   4   5

Rate 1-5 how often you feel like you were consistent with your reps this week

1   2   3   4   5

bject: I'll Have a Grande

I know you all have different types of orders for your
caffeine fix. Some are simple; then there are some of you, I
am sure, are a little more complex.

The great thing is no matter the complexity of your order,
it always comes out the way you ordered it. You can't
order coaches like you order your Starbucks drink. Let's
be honest; Starbucks would be pretty boring if they only
served hot, black coffee. They also probably wouldn't have
over 27,000 locations worldwide.

I know there are a lot of us who wish we could just place
an order for a coach, and poof, there they are in all their
perfectness! But the reality of it is there is always going to
be difficulties when ordering a coach.

So let's look into the different types of coffee coaches, and
their strengths and difficulties:

But, first, we have to understand the three basic
coffee drinks:

Coffee- No explanation needed.

Frappuccino- Blended dessert coffee drinks.

Espresso- These are shots of espresso used as a base to
build upon.

The commonality of the three basic drinks above is the fact
they all come from the coffee bean. Most coaches come
from a similar background in exercise and/or a passion
for helping others. There are some differences between
coaches, which aren't always a bad thing. Baskin Robbins
has thirty-one flavors, not because vanilla wouldn't sell but
it needs a little help.

Understanding the three basic coffee coaches:

The Coffee Coach- This is the *purest* coach.

Strengths: They are bold and full of energy. These are also your *motivators*. They have the uncommon ability to light a spark in people.

Difficulties: They are sometimes bitter, strong-willed, and aren't able to slow things down to appreciate those around them. They could cause a strong case of the gitters.

The Frappuccino Coach- This is the "blended" coach.

Strengths: They are a blend of different coaching styles. They are sweet and give lots of comfort. Aren't afraid to try new ideas and explore their coaching personalities. Strong ability to be a *relator*. They relate because they appeal to the coffee crowd, but also the "non" coffee people who want the caffeine buzz.

Difficulties: They like to live free and don't always have direction. They sometimes can deal with an identity crisis, because they want to be a coffee but act more like a milkshake. They try too many different approaches to their coaching.

The Espresso Coach- This is the IT Coach.

Strengths: They are the fullest expression of the coffee coach, taking the coffee coach to the next level. These coaches have mastered their craft. They are sort of a chameleon and have the ability to morph between the motivator and relator at any given time. They are the smooth operator. Their energy is more of a passion.

Difficulties: These coaches are like unicorns; they are hard to find. Ego is usually a trait they can develop over time. Keeping them once you have them becomes the biggest difficulty.

As the barista (Leader) it's your job to handle these different types of coffee, which will lead to you constantly taking inventory of your coffee. There are three different types of coffee coach inventories you must perform.

First is always making sure you have enough coffee in stock. Like I mentioned earlier you can just order up a coffee coach anytime you want. You always have to be on the lookout for the next premium blend. This ensures you will never miss a beat when your customers come looking for their favorite coffee. Always have a storage room of coach inventory. Never stop interviewing for new brews.

Second is checking for freshness. Coffee is perishable. When left unattended and checked on frequently. Your coaches and can lose those natural flavors and aromas. To prevent this, you should keep tabs on your coach's freshness. Checking one their freshness a minimum of twice a week. Remember members are coming for the energy they get from the coach. If they order a bold coffee and got decaf instead, they are going to start looking for other coffee shops. It's important we are finding ways to keep our coaches fresh and caffeine content high.

Thirdly you will want to gather feedback on your brews. The best place to gather feedback is from the customers/members themselves. Are they ranking their coffee coach experience high. If so they are more likely to share the news with their friends, think of this as a yelp review of your coffee coach.

As we learned it's not just about finding the right type of coffee, each has their strengths and difficulties. You must inventory your coffee constantly.

I would be interested to see if you can identify which of your coaches fits the types above.

Also, which inventory category do you need to put a little more focus on right now?

Free Space to write down key takeaways or answers to any questions found in this week's email:

_____

_____

_____

_____

Questions

Answer any challenging questions the email posed to you:

_____

_____

_____

_____

Challenge

What was the leadership challenge that spoke to you this week?

_____

_____

_____

_____

Perform

How do you plan to perform the challenges this week?

_____

_____

_____

_____

Repetitions

What do you need to do to remind yourself to get your reps in this week?

_____

_____

_____

_____

CPR Progress Report

(1 Needed Major Improvement - 5 CRUSHED IT!)

Rate yourself 1-5 on your leadership challenge this week

1   2   3   4   5

Rate 1-5 how well do you think you performed this week

1   2   3   4   5

Rate 1-5 how often you feel like you were consistent with your reps this week

1   2   3   4   5

Have you ever really taken the time to think about the role of a conductor? It involves much more then waving your arms around like a crazy person.

The responsibility of a conductor is to unify performers, set the tempo, execute clear preparation, listen to the sound of the ensemble, and control the interpretation and pacing of the music.

The conductor is not the best cello, flute, or trombone player, and he isn't responsible for the individual. The conductor has the entire orchestra to unify and manage.

This is much like the *head coach* role. Over the last week, I have spoken to most of you on the phone. One of the main topics was what is a head coach's role? How do I know I am actually doing a good job? Are these the right things I should be doing?

I think we can all take a lesson from the conductor here.

Are you the conductor of your business?

The fitness side of the house is a business like the sales side. Are you:

- Unifying your team

  - Not just developing coaches, but developing the team to be strong as a unit. There is a difference here.

  - Unifying with your manager and support each other. You are both conductors and have to know each other's next note, supporting the next move and unifying both sides of the business.

- Setting the tempo

    - Much like music has a certain tempo, and like base pace, without a conductor (coach), tempo can easily get thrown off.

    - Setting proper tempo for your team's growth and expectations is key in the success of the development of the whole team.

- Listen to the sounds

    - Much like an orchestra, there are many different instruments which are responsible for different sounds. Our business has different instruments (processes/systems) that when we leave some out or don't pay attention to all of them, the sound is distorted.

    - We have our performers, managers, SA's, coaches, members. If we can keep our ears open to the sounds of our performers in our business, we will have a much better idea of how to handle situations when they come up and bring them back into sync!

- Pace your teams

    - If the cello performers are only concerned about their piece, they may not know the trombone's piece because it's not their job. However, they must understand the pace, and that's the conductor's job. If not paced properly, they could end up short.

- We must help pace our coaches and SA's with goals. The coaches may not know what the sales goal is or how close they are unless they are told by you. You have to help keep your teams on pace with where they are and what they need to do to hit goals.

Can you start to be a conductor of your business this week? Think a little bit differently about how to lead.

Subject: CPR Report

Free Space to write down key takeaways or answers to any questions found in this week's email:

_____

_____

_____

_____

Questions

Answer any challenging questions the email posed to you:

_____

_____

_____

_____

Challenge

What was the leadership challenge that spoke to you this week?

_____

_____

_____

_____

Perform

How do you plan to perform the challenges this week?

_____

_____

_____

_____

Repetitions

What do you need to do to remind yourself to get your reps in this week?

_____

_____

_____

_____

CPR Progress Report

(1 Needed Major Improvement - 5 CRUSHED IT!)

Rate yourself 1-5 on your leadership challenge this week

1   2   3   4   5

Rate 1-5 how well do you think you performed this week

1   2   3   4   5

Rate 1-5 how often you feel like you were consistent with your reps this week

1   2   3   4   5

Subject: Pressure Points

We all have them and they are not enjoyable when targeted with pressure. However, I believe there may be a PURPOSE behind the pressure.

See, with privilege comes pressure. We all want certain privileges (like being a head coach or manager), but sometimes aren't ready or don't want the pressure.

Your new privileges of:

- Assisting in running a successful business
- Leading a team
- Creating a rock star culture
- Always being "ON"
- Continual development of staff
- Numbers and reports
- Member concerns/ questions/ complaints
- Longer hours you feel go unnoticed and underappreciated

The list above can start to look overwhelming and become points of pressure.

When the pressure is building, we have to take a deep breath and ask ourselves a few questions:

- How well do I handle pressure?
- Is the pressure pointing out a deficiency?
- Am I able to notice where I need help?

- Are you willing to ask for help?

- Who am I going to ask for help?

Once you have identified the answers to the above questions, you will be better equipped with handling the pressure of your privileges. Pressure points out areas of opportunity, and with that comes continual growth. The growth needed to get you through the next pressure point and a solution when the pressure becomes too much.

Pressure comes into your life not because of what you are handling, but because of how you are handling it. Be willing to seek the advice and ask for help.

Don't be afraid of pressure. Pressure creates beautiful things like diamonds. Understand the purpose of the pressure and learn to grow from it. Pressure will either crush you or turn you into a diamond.

Subject: CPR Report

Free Space to write down key takeaways or answers to any questions found in this week's email:

_____

_____

_____

_____

Questions

Answer any challenging questions the email posed to you:

_____

_____

_____

_____

Challenge

What was the leadership challenge that spoke to you this week?

_____

_____

_____

_____

Perform

How do you plan to perform the challenges this week?

_____

_____

_____

_____

Repetitions

What do you need to do to remind yourself to get your reps in this week?

_____

_____

_____

_____

CPR Progress Report

(1 Needed Major Improvement - 5 CRUSHED IT!)

Rate yourself 1-5 on your leadership challenge this week

1   2   3   4   5

Rate 1-5 how well do you think you performed this week

1   2   3   4   5

Rate 1-5 how often you feel like you were consistent with your reps this week

1   2   3   4   5

Subject: I Don't Clean Toilets

If that's the case, they better always be clean. A guy I worked with at corporate used to say, "*Clean clean things. They never have a chance to get dirty then.*"

But I'm in management. You aren't above it, period. Actually, you should be the first one to grab a cloth and wipe down the bathroom, or clean out that nasty employee fridge that people leave their six-week-old broccoli in. I see this all too often and it drives me absolutely nuts.

At the core of leadership is setting the example or leading by example.

As you know, I have been in fitness for a long time. I would have never asked a client of mine to do an exercise that I haven't done before. I have to be able to experience it before I can coach someone else about how to do it correctly and effectively.

It's no different than a manager or assistant manager or CEO cleaning the bathroom.

Little do you know that small, little act will grow your respect among your team.

That's worth it in itself outside of the clean bathroom.

When I was working for the corporate office, I'll never forget this time I walked into a studio to do an audit. The studio was not in the best shape from a cleanliness point of view. There was a hairball on the weight floor the size of my shoe. I actually put my foot next to it and took a picture for verification. The shower curtains had mold on the liners, and a variety of other problems; we'll say non-compliant hygiene.

I lost so much respect for that manager that day. As we were walking the studio together, I pointed out the huge hairball on the floor. He shrugged his shoulders and did nothing. A few minutes later, I saw one of the coaches come back and sweep it up.

I am so ruined by doing audits because now, everywhere I go, I always look at the ceilings and bathrooms through that lens. I wouldn't suggest looking at those things.

There are two takeaways I want you to grab from the examples above.

The first being the respect of your peers and employees. You can never earn respect until others see you doing the work you are asking. To be honest, the things that seem to go unnoticed are the ones that will earn you the most respect. Think about people you respect. I want you to write two of their names, then I want you to write two reasons you respect them. They probably did something to help you. So you had some personal gain, whether they knew it or not. Or they performed in your eyes a humble act.

I had one of our directors tell me last night that she picked up a few things about how I talk to people. I wasn't trying to teach her; I was just going about my normal routine.

You can't try to earn respect, because then it's not genuine. If you want genuine respect, you must be genuine in work. Don't do it because someone is watching; do it because someone needs help.

Secondly, there was a lack of pride. You know how when you invite people over, you want your house to look good so you clean it. I mean like *really* clean it: get out the good-smelling volcano candles; make sure there aren't any light bulbs out. It's because you are proud of where you live.

Or when you buy a new car. You wash it every day, make sure you throw out all the trash. It's because you are proud of your purchase.

Pride is constant. Constant means a state of affairs that doesn't change. A prime example of pride that isn't constant is that new car example. How long is it before you forget to wash it? Two weeks, two months, two years?

What are you proud of and how do you treat it? Do you take special care of it? Is it something you want to show off to the world? How about where you work? Do you wear your company logo proudly?

One person who comes to mind who is proud of their work is John, our cleaning guy. As most know, this is his second job. He is a high-level manager at one of the large home supply stores. But he loves cleaning because he knows the impact it has on others. When they walk into a studio after he cleans it, you have no idea how much that means to him. He actually asked me when I was doing an audit one day, "What do I need to do to help these studios rock these audits?" I gave him a few items and, to this day, he always does them; and still always asks how he can improve the cleaning. Man, he is the definition of being proud of his work.

The more pride you carry with you about your studio, it will catch on and others will become more proud of the studio.

Your teams are looking up to you, always watching. Where do you need to inject a little pride into your studio? What act or acts do you need to perform to continue to earn the respect of your team?

bject: CPR Report

Free Space to write down key takeaways or answers to any questions found in this week's email:

_____

_____

_____

_____

Questions

Answer any challenging questions the email posed to you:

_____

_____

_____

_____

Challenge

What was the leadership challenge that spoke to you this week?

_____

_____

_____

_____

Perform

How do you plan to perform the challenges this week?

_____

_____

_____

_____

Repetitions

What do you need to do to remind yourself to get your reps in this week?

_____

_____

_____

_____

CPR Progress Report

(1 Needed Major Improvement - 5 CRUSHED IT!)

Rate yourself 1-5 on your leadership challenge this week

1   2   3   4   5

Rate 1-5 how well do you think you performed this week

1   2   3   4   5

Rate 1-5 how often you feel like you were consistent with your reps this week

1   2   3   4   5

bject: Details

I know why you opened this... you probably thought this
was for a meeting update or a phone call that I was going to
make you get on. Well, what if I told you, you were wrong?
I'm talking about a different type of detail; the details
that set apart your business and make members want to
stay for life.

These are the type of details you don't see because your
lens is a little foggy, like when you go from the AC to the
humid Florida heat.

I'm talking about the devil that's in the details. You know
you have heard that idiom before, but how have you
interrupted it? I think it's fun how everyone can see it a little
differently.

I believe the "devil" is the missing element in the details.
What little hidden details are you missing in your business,
your member experience, your day-to-day routine,
your effort?

What I want you to do tomorrow, or the very next time you
step into your studio, is:

- Look at the details in

  - Cleanliness

  - Friendliness

  - Liveliness

- Now observe

  - Staff-to-staff interactions

  - Staff-to-member interactions

  - Member-to-member interactions

- Lastly, check

  - Your attitude

  - Your team's attitude

  - Your studio's attitude

Think about this: DETAILS create MOMENTS, and MOMENTS create MEMORIES.

Take a second and reflect on a recent memory that exceeded your expectation.

Write out:

- What were the details that exceeded your expectations?

- What moments couldn't have been replicated anywhere else?

- What specific memories have you carried with you from that experience?

Let's look at the mysterious, missing details in our business and studios this week. Let's create a plan on how we can exceed our members' expectations. By over-delivering on the details and creating moments they will talk to their friends about, we will build memories for a lifetime.

CPR Report

Free Space to write down key takeaways or answers to any questions found in this week's email:

_____

_____

_____

_____

Questions

Answer any challenging questions the email posed to you:

_____

_____

_____

_____

Challenge

What was the leadership challenge that spoke to you this week?

_____

_____

_____

_____

Perform

How do you plan to perform the challenges this week?

_____

_____

_____

_____

Repetitions

What do you need to do to remind yourself to get your reps in this week?

_____

_____

_____

_____

CPR Progress Report

(1 Needed Major Improvement - 5 CRUSHED IT!)

Rate yourself 1-5 on your leadership challenge this week

1   2   3   4   5

Rate 1-5 how well do you think you performed this week

1   2   3   4   5

Rate 1-5 how often you feel like you were consistent with your reps this week

1   2   3   4   5

With the subject line, you are probably expecting me to give you some secrets of how to magically increase your sales, or find a hundred more leads, or pack every single one of your classes, so your coaches are happy. Nah, not really... it actually has nothing to do with any of the above.

I experienced a WOW moment this week I wanted to share with you all. Then I have one of my famous acronyms for you.

Okay, so by now, you have stopped reading because this isn't helpful for you. Well, just hang on a second; let me have a chance to be a little vulnerable with you.

This past week, I have:

Seen, heard, observed, and talked to many members and staff (one on one). It made me self-reflect a little bit about where my head is as the bus driver of this organization. This brought me back to the rules of the Energy Bus:

- You're the driver of your bus.
- Desire, vision, and focus move your bus in the right direction.
- Fuel your ride with positive energy.
- Invite people on your bus and share your vision for the road ahead.
- Don't waste your energy on those who don't get on your bus.
- Post a sign that says "No Energy Vampires Allowed" on your bus.

- Enthusiasm attracts more passengers and energized them during the ride.

- Love your passengers.

- Drive with purpose.

- Have fun and enjoy the ride.

I would encourage you to think about these rules and determine if you are following at least eight of the ten.

When I reflect on the previous month, and even the week sometimes, I know where I have opportunities for improvement. Each one of these rules will help you reflect on your motives and purpose.

I am so excited about being re-focused and energized with these rules in mind. I would challenge you to write or print these out. Put them somewhere you will see them first thing in the morning. Focus on two of them each day this week.

I know what you're thinking: *"How does that have anything to do with REAP?"* Just hang on and keep reading.

The WOW moment I had this week was two words: satisfaction and loyalty. I want to start by saying you truly REAP what you sow.

This week, I would like you to take a moment and R.E.A.P. with your teams.

Recognize

- Give out a weekly award or a month award for someone you felt went above and beyond for the studio or a member.

- Do this not only privately but publicly.

Encourage

- Is there someone on your team who could use a one-on-one over a cup of coffee?

- Encouragement doesn't only come in the form of pushing to achieve. It's also relational.

Appreciate

- Think of three ways you can appreciate your team this week.

- Maybe you can bring their favorite energy drinks or candy; maybe write them a card.

Prepare

- Spend some time developing someone.

- Help them prepare for the month to come. March Mania, our regional contest, and the March promotions are coming up.

If you sow in these areas above, you will REAP x10.

Also, team, as we get read to close out February, I have updated the Core 4 scoreboard and attached it to this email.

Please review and set some goals for the week.

Subject: CPR Report

Free Space to write down key takeaways or answers to any questions found in this week's email:

_____
_____
_____
_____

Questions

Answer any challenging questions the email posed to you:

_____
_____
_____
_____

Challenge

What was the leadership challenge that spoke to you this week?

_____
_____
_____
_____

Perform

How do you plan to perform the challenges this week?

_____

_____

_____

_____

Repetitions

What do you need to do to remind yourself to get your reps in this week?

_____

_____

_____

_____

CPR Progress Report

(1 Needed Major Improvement - 5 CRUSHED IT!)

Rate yourself 1-5 on your leadership challenge this week

1   2   3   4   5

Rate 1-5 how well do you think you performed this week

1   2   3   4   5

Rate 1-5 how often you feel like you were consistent with your reps this week

1   2   3   4   5

Subject: OmaHA OmaNA or Maybe…

Is it Time to Call an Audible in Your Studio?

Watching some of the games today reminded me of the art of calling an audible. The key to the audible is clear vision with a desired outcome.

Quarterbacks can see things at the line of scrimmage that may cause them to call an audible. This is to help their offense outsmart and outplay the defense on that play.

As the quarterback of your business, you have to understand the "art" of the audible.

I'll keep it really simple for you: All you have to remember is S.A.P.P. (named after one of the greats, defensive linemen Warren Sapp.)

Skilled

- Skilled at reading their environment.
- Skilled at reading their staff.
- Skilled at reading their forecast.
- Skilled at reading their competitors

Awareness

- Aware of subtle changes.
- Aware of their team's morale.
- Aware of their key players.
- Aware of the pressure.

Plan

- They have pre-planned alternative scenarios.
- They have a plan for the predicted scenarios.
- They have a plan for continuing to keep their team motivated and inspired no matter the scenario.
- They have a plan for overcoming every scenario.

Posture

- Their posture is cool under pressure.
- Their posture is always positive.
- Their posture is strong.
- Their posture causes others to be more confident.

With each of the above four bullet points in the SAPP Audible list, which ones can you check off as being done and taken care of?

Where could you call an audible? If you need to Omaha, which bullet point do you think is most needed to get a first down?

I want you to write down what a first down looks like for you and your team.

I also want you to write down what a touchdown looks like for you and your team.

Know and understand those key points on how we can consistently advance with first downs, while ultimately converting every drive.

Subject: CPR Report

Free Space to write down key takeaways or answers to any questions found in this week's email:

_____

_____

_____

_____

Questions

Answer any challenging questions the email posed to you:

_____

_____

_____

Challenge

What was the leadership challenge that spoke to you this week?

_____

_____

_____

_____

Perform

How do you plan to perform the challenges this week?

_____

_____

_____

_____

Repetitions

What do you need to do to remind yourself to get your reps in this week?

_____

_____

_____

_____

CPR Progress Report

(1 Needed Major Improvement - 5 CRUSHED IT!)

Rate yourself 1-5 on your leadership challenge this week

1   2   3   4   5

Rate 1-5 how well do you think you performed this week

1   2   3   4   5

Rate 1-5 how often you feel like you were consistent with your reps this week

1   2   3   4   5

Subject: **Better Tasting**

STOP Rouge! This is a daily occurrence lately in my house. Rouge is our almost seven-year-old labradoodle. He is constantly trying to eat our older dogs' soft food. He is on soft food because of his old teeth. I guess it tastes better. It's interesting to me to watch this and see this over and over again.

Rouge by no means is starving! He has his own food and it's not cheap food. Although he will take the risk of getting yelled at for the chance to steal Diesel's food.

This got me thinking of that old saying the "grass is green". People are always looking for "better tasting food" until they realize it ends up doing the same thing. It fills the void of hunger. It may taste a little better going down but guess what. Your stomach doesn't know a $5 steak vs. a $100 A5 Wagyu steak. It's just the initial 30 seconds that steak enters your body you can taste the difference. However, it takes about four hours for your body to digest that steak. The long-term process is still the same. It doesn't matter how appetizing that new food looks or smells. At the end of the day once the sensation of smell and taste are gone. The process is still the same. There will always be a digestion process that happens. With any new job or opportunity there will always be processes and systems. Better tasting food doesn't change processes or systems. If you struggle with processes that Wagyu taste will quickly become foul.

Too many people are like Rouge. They are willing to give up what they have for a possibly better tasting opportunity. When at the end of the day that food will also become just food that fills you up and no longer satisfies your taste buds.

I know there are a lot of people who have been looking for "greener" grass in this last year. I will tell you this, the grass is always greener until you start to play on it. Then it becomes worn down and dirty just like the grass you were previously on.

Why do people look for a better tasting food or greener grass? It's a great question to begin to unpack and look at. I am not an expert in the physiological reasons people are looking for other opportunities. All I can share is from my experience. More importantly I want to give you some actionable ways to avoid looking for better tasting food.

I believe there are three reasons people look for better looking/tasting opportunities:

A Mirage of hope- I saw a quote, "The grass is green on the other side, because it's fake grass." Just like a mirage is fake. Why do Mirages happen? Because you become desperate for something and begin to see those things in the distance. Better question: why do you lose hope? Because you start to lose a sense of expectation and desired outcome. Sometimes on the grass you are standing on will cause you to lose hope, because you lost gratitude for your current situation. When you begin to lose gratitude for where you are and what you have. You will begin to see a Mirage of hope. The greener grass looks like all the things you want, the desired outcomes you don't think you will have where you currently are. The mirage will only show you what's missing from your current situation.

How do you avoid a Mirage of Hope

- Rehydrate yourself with gratitude.
- List out the top 10 things you are grateful for in your current situation. Put them on your desk.

A Lack of growth- Another quote I saw, "The grass is greener where you water it." Currently in my neighborhood there are some people's grass that is greener than others. I was getting frustrated because mine doesn't look so hot. Until I talked to Faith, and she said, "well are we watering ours, because I have seen others starting to water theirs?" I thought to myself well nope we aren't right now! See it's my fault my grass isn't getting greener. I am in total control of my grasses ability to get green. Like many others we lose sight of our grass because we are looking at everyone else's.

How to avoid a lack of growth

- Grab a hose and start to water

- Stop comparing your grass to others especially when you haven't taken to proper steps to make yours greener.

A vision problem- You feel trapped by an imaginary fence. The grass you are standing on may not be as green as the other grass. This is because you are not restricted with your movement where you are. You have the freedom to explore and move around. Which could cause some wear and tear in the pasture. You have freedom and area to grow where you are. But it doesn't always look as pretty as the other grass over there. What you don't see is the reason the grass is greener over there. There is an underground electric fence. The grass is greener because of restricted movement. Once you get to that patch you can't move anywhere else so you stay put. Because you are afraid to move and don't want to get shocked! You stop exploring the new territory and became paralyzed by fear.

How do you fix a vision problem?

- Avoid the appeal of what you can see, because what you can't see may get you shocked.

- Instead, explore the territory you have. Look for a path to success in the steps of those who were there before you.

Are you feeling like you need some better tasting food?

Is there a mirage in front of you?

Do you need to rehydrate with some gratitude?

Is there a kink in your hose? How do you plan to make your grass greener?

Have you been shocked by an opportunity that looked better?

Is there a better path where you currently are that you have found yet?

I am happy to help anyone with finding the answers to the above questions this week!

Let's have an awesome week!

Subject: CPR Report

Free Space to write down key takeaways or answers to any questions found in this week's email:

_____

_____

_____

_____

Questions

Answer any challenging questions the email posed to you:

_____

_____

_____

_____

Challenge

What was the leadership challenge that spoke to you this week?

_____

_____

_____

_____

Perform

How do you plan to perform the challenges this week?

_____

_____

_____

_____

Repetitions

What do you need to do to remind yourself to get your reps in this week?

_____

_____

_____

_____

CPR Progress Report

(1 Needed Major Improvement - 5 CRUSHED IT!)

Rate yourself 1-5 on your leadership challenge this week

1   2   3   4   5

Rate 1-5 how well do you think you performed this week

1   2   3   4   5

Rate 1-5 how often you feel like you were consistent with your reps this week

1   2   3   4   5

Subject: Leaders Love

Love, when you hear that you probably think about the first time you laid eyes on what is now your spouse. Just like all the movies love is such a simple thing, right? NO! Love is really easy when things are new and going well. Love becomes difficult when it's not exciting anymore or it seems like the same old routine. Just like love should lead your relationships, you should lead with love at work.

Leaders love what they do and who they work with...or at least they should.

But do we lead with love? When I think of love, I think of wedding ceremonies. There is a couple who are, no doubt, in love and make it publicly known by standing there taking their vows.

During a wedding, there is usually someone who reads about what love is:

- Patient
- Kind
- Protects
- Trusts
- Hopes
- Preserves
- Never Fails

I don't think these characteristics of love are too much different than leading others. This goes for our coaches and our members.

Over the next three weeks, I am going to take a deeper dive into each one of these characteristics. We will discover how we can use them to become better leaders, along with giving some action steps on how to implement these into our daily practice of leading a team.

Leading with Patience:

- Allow opportunity for mistakes. Humans will make mistakes and that's perfectly okay. Sometimes what's not okay is our expectations when it comes to making mistakes. As a leader, I am sure there are times you have made mistakes.

- When I think about having patience, sports come to mind. Some of the greatest games are won in the last two minutes. However, if you aren't leading your team into those moments with patience, you are actually creating panic. With patience comes success, even when it's a hurry-up situation.

- John Wooden said, "When we are patient, we'll have a greater appreciation of our success." Take time to lead and develop with patience, and greater success will follow.

Things to think about this week:

- Do you have a new employee or team member? Are you allowing them space and freedom to make mistakes before you put them in the big game? How many times do we, out of desperation, put in the rookie, and expect them to win the game without them knowing the full playbook? They haven't messed up enough yet. How many times do you have to mess up before you get it right? The answer is, it's different for everyone, which is where your patience comes in.

- Don't get frustrated; find fulfillment in the process of being patient.

- Apply small, daily learning with your team. Fire Drill cards are a great way to do this. You don't have to fix everything today.

- Are you creating panic in the last two minutes with your team? Or, are you poised and does your team look to you for confidence in times of panic?

- If you are looking for quick success in your business, employees, or personal development, then go back to sleep and keep dreaming. Success will come with large doses of patience and consistency. If you lead knowing this, then your whole team, business, and outlook will take a dramatic turn.

Next week, we will dive into being kind.

bject: CPR Report

Free Space to write down key takeaways or answers to any questions found in this week's email:

_____

_____

_____

_____

Questions

Answer any challenging questions the email posed to you:

_____

_____

_____

_____

Challenge

What was the leadership challenge that spoke to you this week?

_____

_____

_____

_____

Perform

How do you plan to perform the challenges this week?

_____

_____

_____

_____

Repetitions

What do you need to do to remind yourself to get your reps in this week?

_____

_____

_____

_____

CPR Progress Report

(1 Needed Major Improvement - 5 CRUSHED IT!)

Rate yourself 1-5 on your leadership challenge this week

1   2   3   4   5

Rate 1-5 how well do you think you performed this week

1   2   3   4   5

Rate 1-5 how often you feel like you were consistent with your reps this week

1   2   3   4   5

bject: Oh, You're so Kind

By opening this, you probably thought a couple of different things. This is another of Heath's tricks in getting me to open his email... is this another SPAM email from Heath? Or what does Heath need that I might be able to help? If you chose the third option, then you are one step closer to leading with love.

In week two of our *Lead with Love* series, we are talking about how to be kind when leading. Leadership = Protection.

Be Kind When Leading:

- Don't mistake kindness for weakness.

- Kindness as a leader is being generous and considerate. This especially applies when providing feedback and developmental moments.

  - Be considerate of what I call the three Ts of feedback: Timing/ Tone/ Transparency

  - Be generous to those on your team who go above and beyond. Being generous doesn't always have to be monetary.

- Kindness is at the root of each one of us. It's up to you if you want to use it while being a leader. A large element of being a leader is getting people to follow you because they like you. This is one characteristic that will help you win over this level of leadership.

Leadership = Protection:

- Typically, people we care for we protect. People put security in those they feel look out for them.

- I know you all have friends in your life who've you got their back; those *Ride or Die* friends. Your staff is looking for the same type of investment from you for them.

- If your staff knows they come first, they will want to perform their best for you.

- Protection means keeping their best interests at hand.

- Protection enhances confidence, like a quarterback has confidence in his line to protect him from the defense. When your staff feels you are looking out for them, this will help increase their level of confidence not only in themselves, but you as a leader as well.

bject: CPR Report

Free Space to write down key takeaways or answers to any questions found in this week's email:

_____

_____

_____

_____

Questions

Answer any challenging questions the email posed to you:

_____

_____

_____

_____

Challenge

What was the leadership challenge that spoke to you this week?

_____

_____

_____

_____

Perform

How do you plan to perform the challenges this week?

_____

_____

_____

_____

Repetitions

What do you need to do to remind yourself to get your reps in this week?

_____

_____

_____

_____

CPR Progress Report

(1 Needed Major Improvement - 5 CRUSHED IT!)

Rate yourself 1-5 on your leadership challenge this week

1   2   3   4   5

Rate 1-5 how well do you think you performed this week

1   2   3   4   5

Rate 1-5 how often you feel like you were consistent with your reps this week

1   2   3   4   5

What's next?

If you have ever felt yourself asking these questions, how do you think your team is feeling?

They look to you for hope and trust that you have the next steps already figured out.

In week three of the *Lead with Love* series, I want to dive a little deeper into what it means to lead with hope and why trust is so important.

You know what I love about sports this time of year? Every week matters now as we get closer to the playoffs. Every week you hope that your team is going to leave with a W! But what you are really hoping for is that they prepared for this week's game. See, a lot of times, hope is placed in what you can't see. If you were there all week at their practice, team meetings, film sessions, and scouting report reviews, you would trust that they have done the work to prepare. But the reality is most of us just hope that our team isn't going to let us down week after week.

Project Hope:

- Hope is a feeling of expectation and desire for certain things to happen.

- Napoleon said: "A leader is a dealer in hope." Leaders have to be able to inspire a sense of expectation inside of their teams and organizations.

- Just like you, hoping your team put in the work to win the game, your team also hopes that you are putting in the work to help them grow, develop, and become more successful.

- A good leader shares vision and sets expectations for success. But again, a lot of this work goes on behind closed doors that our teams do not always see. But they hope you are following through with your promises. Don't let your team's hope in you fade.

- Hope can be easily robbed but not easily gained.

Trust me:

- One of the most important elements of leadership is trust. Without trust, you will never be able to build a team.

- Like hope, trust is fragile. It takes a long time to build and seconds to break.

- Trusting you as a leader is your team's decision. Proving them right is up to you. Trust is all about putting your money where your mouth is.

- Getting a trust by-in is a huge bump in your leadership score. This by-in comes from past experiences in your industry, your credibility in your current role, consistently being a trustful resource, etc. People trust those who have performed well on a high level in their industry. More importantly, they start to believe it when they can see it.

- Lastly, your team has to trust you have what's best for them and not yourself. Trust is all about being a servant-based leader.

bject: **CPR Report**

Free Space to write down key takeaways or answers to any questions found in this week's email:

_____

_____

_____

_____

Questions

Answer any challenging questions the email posed to you:

_____

_____

_____

_____

Challenge

What was the leadership challenge that spoke to you this week?

_____

_____

_____

_____

Perform

How do you plan to perform the challenges this week?

_____

_____

_____

_____

Repetitions

What do you need to do to remind yourself to get your reps in this week?

_____

_____

_____

_____

CPR Progress Report

(1 Needed Major Improvement - 5 CRUSHED IT!)

Rate yourself 1-5 on your leadership challenge this week

1   2   3   4   5

Rate 1-5 how well do you think you performed this week

1   2   3   4   5

Rate 1-5 how often you feel like you were consistent with your reps this week

1   2   3   4   5

bject: What's a Green Thumb?

"A natural talent for growing plants."

A quick backstory for you.

I have been doing some planting recently at my house, which is not something I am very familiar with. I have learned there are certain plants that stay bloomed all year round, and there are others that only bloom annually. There are some which require more sun and some that require less. Others do well only in pots and some that flourish in the ground.

This whole process has taught me a few lessons that I would like to translate into terms of leadership.

See, I believe there are two types of leaders: developers and directors.

Developers see the landscape, which they are working with. They are able to stand outside the picture frame and see the larger picture. They are able to see potential, possibility, and capabilities, which will help them better understand how to grow and develop.

Directors expect the landscaping to already be finished. The bigger picture is hard for them to see because they are living in the frame. They sometimes cannot see potential, possibility, or capabilities. Their observations are often skewed by accusations, which prohibits development and growth.

See, when you get plants home from the store, they should be ready to put in the ground. However, this does require a little work on your end. You have to find the right spot with sun and rain but not too much, only what's required. You will need to prepare the ground. To do that, you will need certain lawn tools.

All of the above steps are what a developer expects before they take on a project. Directors will already expect these steps are done ahead of time.

Differences Between Developers and Directors:

- Developers know they must use the tool to prepare the soil to give the plant the best situation to grow. A director will lay the tools by the plant and expect it to dig its own hole.

- Developers also know you must continue to check on your plants frequently to make sure they are getting enough sunlight and rain, and if not, they will water them. Directors expect the plants will grow on their own and get their own sunlight and rain.

- Developers take the time to add fertilizer, knowing this is going to grow the plant faster, but also to grow it stronger. Directors use fertilizer, but they use it to try and accelerate growth in hopes of less work on their end.

- Developers trust in their work and the process. Directors are skeptical of their plants' abilities.

Answer these questions honestly and really evaluate your responses:

- Are you able to see the bigger picture?

- Are you able to share that vision with your staff?

- Do you lay the groundwork of development before you provide feedback?

- Or, do you rush right into feedback, because we want our coaches to be the best overnight?

- Do you approach development with empathy?

- Or, do you approach development with a mallet?

Do you trust your coaches, their abilities, and are you optimistic?

Subject: CPR Report

Free Space to write down key takeaways or answers to any questions found in this week's email:

_____
_____
_____
_____

Questions

Answer any challenging questions the email posed to you:

_____
_____
_____
_____

Challenge

What was the leadership challenge that spoke to you this week?

_____
_____
_____
_____

Perform

How do you plan to perform the challenges this week?

_____

_____

_____

_____

Repetitions

What do you need to do to remind yourself to get your reps
in this week?

_____

_____

_____

_____

CPR Progress Report

(1 Needed Major Improvement - 5 CRUSHED IT!)

Rate yourself 1-5 on your leadership challenge this week

1   2   3   4   5

Rate 1-5 how well do you think you performed this week

1   2   3   4   5

Rate 1-5 how often you feel like you were consistent with
your reps this week

1   2   3   4   5

Subject: Three Hundred Seconds

Do you think you can effectively train staff in 300 seconds? Yes!

Okay, you probably think I have completely lost it. Everyone, wrap it up; Heath has gone nuts. He is telling me that I can train my staff in 300 seconds.

Well... if you let me finish, and you still think I am nuts, then we'll talk. Did you even take the time to figure out how long 300 seconds is?

No? It's five minutes! That's it, five minutes is all it takes to train your staff. There is some small print to this, though.

Let me explain.

I am not talking about a brand-new, started-yesterday employee. I am talking about current employees who work for you. You know the ones you forget about and take for granted. The ones who show up and, after a while, go through the motions of their jobs. They are also the ones we get frustrated with, but don't give them a hall pass like we do for our newer employees. You say, "They should know better," or, "I expect more." How 'bout, "I can't believe they missed that sale."

Let me ask you; when was the last time you sat down to find out where they need support? You would probably be surprised by the answers.

Now, most of you know me and I love a training opportunity, and sometimes mine last more than five minutes. For you, they don't have to. Think about the Fire Drill cards we have. When was the last time you walked in, said *hi* to your team, and gave them a fist bump? Then you handed them a Fire Drill card about overcoming an objection?

This is designed to be a five-minute training exchange. I have been using Fire Drill cards now for a long time. I love how quick they are. It also forces quick thinking on the part of the employee being quizzed; especially in our world, it doesn't matter whether you are on the sales side or the coaching side. We need people who can think quickly to overcome objections and quickly solve member problems.

Why five minutes? There are two really good reasons I have found five minutes is the sweet spot.

First, let's look at some research. I looked up about how long you have someone's attention while teaching/ training them.

Researchers looked at lapses of attention. They had students press a clicker when they would experience a lapse of attention. First, they measured how long the lapse would last. Most frequently was a minute or less. Secondly, the lapses occurred more frequently than previously thought. They found a frequent lapse after about thirty seconds in, suggesting a settling in time. Then the next spike occurred 4.5 to 5.5 minutes, the next at 7-9 minutes, and next, 9-10 minutes.

Knowing that we all have shorter attention spans nowadays, we need to be able to get down to the nitty gritty quicker. Think about those staff meetings that were an hour long. How many people were actually tuned in? Not because it wasn't great content, but because they can't help but drift on to other topics in their brains. I have found that I have a much better chance of keeping them engaged for at least five minutes.

Which leads me to my second point: I love the accumulative effect of five minutes five times per week. That's twenty-five minutes per week, 100 minutes per month. If you are consistent with this for an entire year, your employees can expect 1,300 minutes of extra development from you. If you are only doing a staff training once a month, that's twelve hours a year that your team is getting training. Compare that to five minutes five times a day at twenty-one hours per year. If you then do the one-hour per month staff training, you will be looking at thirty-three hours. Five minutes is also very doable for the manager and the employee. I like to set objectives we can easily achieve. Because, when it's doable, we are more likely to be consistent with them.

The importance of continual training is better-prepared staffs; less turnover because employees feel supported and valued. They don't feel overwhelmed and underprepared. More confident employees are more effective employees. We also end up spending less money and time training new employees.

Your challenge this week is to write down for Monday-Friday what your five-minute Fire Drill will be with your teams. This will help you stay on track. Then what I want you to do is write down how each employee performed. You may have to go back and provide a little one-on-one time at a later point in the week if you see a need.

bject: CPR Report

Free Space to write down key takeaways or answers to any questions found in this week's email:

_____

_____

_____

_____

Questions

Answer any challenging questions the email posed to you:

_____

_____

_____

_____

Challenge

What was the leadership challenge that spoke to you this week?

_____

_____

_____

_____

Perform

How do you plan to perform the challenges this week?

_____

_____

_____

_____

Repetitions

What do you need to do to remind yourself to get your reps in this week?

_____

_____

_____

_____

CPR Progress Report

(1 Needed Major Improvement - 5 CRUSHED IT!)

Rate yourself 1-5 on your leadership challenge this week

1   2   3   4   5

Rate 1-5 how well do you think you performed this week

1   2   3   4   5

Rate 1-5 how often you feel like you were consistent with your reps this week

1   2   3   4   5

bject: That Loving Feeling

I can remember back to both times I decided to do second grade. Yes, it was a choice! Every year around February 14th there would always be a valentine card exchange! Man I got so pumped for this! It's funny I was actually talking to brother number 3 of mine the other day and my three-year nephew Maverick was in the background telling me how he got Star Wars and Spider-Man Valentine's Day cards. He was so excited. Now if my nephew lived a little closer, I would teach him the art I learned at an early age of picking the right card for the right lucky lady. But that is a lesson for my brother to teach!

I can remember sitting there and scanning through the different cards and saying to try to pick the right card for the right person. You know that Valentine's Day cards are not ONE SIZE fits all sweatpants! OH NO!

Just like how others receive love or are shown appreciation. This is not a one size fits all. I remember when I first met Faith. Which by the way I found the perfect Aladdin Valentine's Day cards for her! Anyways I'll stop telling you all my V-day secrets and get to the point. I would pick her up for dates and give her a compliment like WOW you look amazing! She wouldn't really react! I was like hmmm is that not good enough. I'm pretty loud so maybe she didn't hear me! Or maybe she didn't like what she was wearing! As guys, we never sometimes know the right thing to do or say to make some feel appreciated.

Like being a leader sometimes showing appreciation is hard. You don't always know what to say, what to do, how to say it, how often it should be done. So sometimes that leads to a depressed culture inside your studio.

Which I believe is where we can take a lesson for the great book The 5 Love Languages. It wasn't till after reading this book I understood why Faith didn't respond to what's called words of affirmation. It's because her love language is acts of service.

The 5 love languages aren't just for those in an intimate relationship. It's for all relationships. Instead of love think appreciation.

There are 5 different love languages:

- Acts of service
- Words of affirmation
- Quality time
- Gifts
- Physical touch

I believe once you figure out which style of appreciation your team prefers. You will build a better connection with them and learn how to communicate your appreciation more effectively.

Let's quickly break these down and relate them to the leader team member relationship.

Acts of service First this should be done in my opinion selflessly. Not selfish trying to prove a point. Acts of service would be helping a front desk team member clean while they finish a contact log. Or if they did a great job on the first part of their shift doing the rest of their calls for them. While the coach is stretching the class start cleaning for them. What if you found out your teammate had a flat tire and had to Uber to work. Maybe offer to give them a ride home or offer to pay for their Uber back. These don't have to be big ticket items. They don't always require a lot of effort.

Words of affirmation this is where you can encourage and motivate each other. This in my opinion is the most abused of them all. Because it's easy! Don't get trapped by the lure of convenience! At the same time it's just as easily forgotten. When was the last time you told one of your team members you were proud of them, you know how powerful those words are?! Very!! Affirmation is like dopamine though quick high then the crash. This is why when you used to grab the brown paper lunch bag that you decorated for V-Day and tried to compete with who got the most cards. You were driven by that affirmation. But you forgot by the next day.

Quality Time I love this one in the workplace. This is actually my personal love language. Think about quality time in your studio. This can be taking time to further develop your team, taking them out to grab a coffee and chat, a team outing like a night out at top golf or putt putt, laser tag! Spending time giving up the one currency none of us get back time. I believe the greatest act of showing value is giving up your time for someone else

Gifts we would think this would be the top of everyone list. Everyone likes receiving gifts right? WRONG! We did an internal survey and of most you remember gifts as an incentive was not the top of the list. However, there are individuals that this speaks very loudly to them. When they receive a gift unexpectedly they feel appreciated. You know how our new members receive that really cool coffee mug week 2 of them being with us? That's an unexpected wow moment. Even if your love language isn't gifts, you still feel appreciated when you get it. So take the time and think about how you can wow your team members with an unexpected gift.

Physical Touch NO I'm not suggesting any touching here! However, I do want to explain the power of a high five or a fist bump. Did you know April 15th 2021 is national high five day? There was a study done of NBA teams who gave out high fives; those teams were successful, but the teams that gave out high fives whether they scored or not were more successful. I know you have been in a situation where you wanted to perform so well you got a high five or a fist bump! There is so much power behind it. Have you ever seen the teacher who has a different handshake for each student in his classroom? There is power in that gesture. Even though we are in the era of covid, we can still find ways that personal touch can be effective! I'll give you a quick example. I had yet to meet our new coach who moved for DC. She was coaching at the studio I was about to leave from for a meeting. Before I left I wrote her a little note, it said "Allie have an awesome night of coaching Heath". That is an example of a personal touch that doesn't require hand sanitizer! Find ways to use the power of the personal touch this week.

Finding your love language will also help you understand how you feel appreciated! It's important to know yourself!

bject: **CPR Report**

Free Space to write down key takeaways or answers to any questions found in this week's email:

_____

_____

_____

_____

Questions

Answer any challenging questions the email posed to you:

_____

_____

_____

_____

Challenge

What was the leadership challenge that spoke to you this week?

_____

_____

_____

_____

Perform

How do you plan to perform the challenges this week?

_____

_____

_____

_____

Repetitions

What do you need to do to remind yourself to get your reps in this week?

_____

_____

_____

_____

CPR Progress Report

(1 Needed Major Improvement - 5 CRUSHED IT!)

Rate yourself 1-5 on your leadership challenge this week

1   2   3   4   5

Rate 1-5 how well do you think you performed this week

1   2   3   4   5

Rate 1-5 how often you feel like you were consistent with your reps this week

1   2   3   4   5

bject: Tactical

Take a second and think about this word. Now write down
what you *think* tactical means before you continue reading
this email.

Most of us, what probably comes to mind is military special
forces. The definition is:

relating to or constituting actions carefully planned to gain a
specific military end.

So you would be correct if this was what you were thinking.
I have a different idea of the word. I think tactical means
giving yourself a vantage point for success.

When planning for missions, these groups take a very
tactical approach. Careful planning and recon go into these
plans. These Spec Ops groups are not the ones who design
the plans; they are the ones who carry them out.

To complete the mission successfully, they carry different
types of tactical gear for different situations. I wanted to
share with you the OTF Head Coaches Tactical Gear.

Binoculars:

To be able to see in all situations, they must have some
sort of visual advantage; not only being able to see from
a distance but having a clear vision. When it comes to the
Head Coach Binoculars, you not only need to be able to see
what's happening in your studio when you are there, but also
having a clear vision of how your business is operating when
you are not there. This comes by having a shared vision with
all your coaches and their buy-in, to not only the company
vision but your studio vision as well. Example: If you have

a coach who doesn't see the value in switching a 2G to a 3G and consistently does that, maybe they are not looking through the same binoculars as the rest of the team.

Compass:

The compass is very important to the team's success in execution. If you have no idea of where your end goal is, then you likely will never achieve it. Knowing exactly which direction all your coaches are going in. Think of each one having a different X on a map, and it's your job to correctly guide them to get there. Example: You cannot, nor do you want to, mold each coach after yourself. Each one has different strengths in his/her coaching. It's your job to guide them in the areas of opportunities, which will be different for all your coaches.

Radio:

This is the lifeline literally for the teams on the ground. They must be able to communicate with their team back at command center in case there is something unknown that pops up. Command center then must quickly adjust to continue the team on the road to success. Communication is the bloodline for our studios; when communication breaks down, so does business. We lose members, employees, and, most importantly, our vision. How often do you effectively communicate with your teams? I'm not talking just meeting; I mean truly meaningful communication, which leaves your employee saying, "Wow, they really do care about me!"

I want to challenge you this week to take these three tactical items with you to work and every day, write down one thing you either did, or experienced, for each item. At the end of the week, I promise you will learn something. I will be reaching out to all of you to find out what you learned.

Free Space to write down key takeaways or answers to any questions found in this week's email:

_____

_____

_____

_____

Questions

Answer any challenging questions the email posed to you:

_____

_____

_____

_____

Challenge

What was the leadership challenge that spoke to you this week?

_____

_____

_____

_____

Perform

How do you plan to perform the challenges this week?

_____

_____

_____

_____

Repetitions

What do you need to do to remind yourself to get your reps in this week?

_____

_____

_____

_____

CPR Progress Report

(1 Needed Major Improvement - 5 CRUSHED IT!)

Rate yourself 1-5 on your leadership challenge this week

1   2   3   4   5

Rate 1-5 how well do you think you performed this week

1   2   3   4   5

Rate 1-5 how often you feel like you were consistent with your reps this week

1   2   3   4   5

Have you ever felt like there is a scarcity of development happening in your studios? Why do you think that is? I know it can be frustrating, and you may feel helpless, angry, beside yourself. Well, I want you to think about this phrase I wrote down this morning, as I was thinking about this topic.

"Is the scarcity of development because of a shortage of supply?"

I started thinking about how leaders pour into their staff. Sometimes there isn't any more to pour. The demand may be greater than the experience of the leader in that position, which is fine; everyone has a deficit. It's not about your deficit; it's how you increase your supply and fill the void.

If you are ready to increase your supply, I am going to give you two quick tips you can start tomorrow.

1. Find a Mentor- This is an easy one. Coming up in the fitness industry, I always had mentors, and they changed based on what season of growth I was in. Some were fitness gurus, some were business gurus, and most of the mentors I had were from other industries. A big network of like-minded individuals who want to see each other succeed is also great to have. There is always something that can be learned from others' experience. Ask yourself this question: *What did I learn today from the people I interact with daily?* If you aren't being filled, find another mentor.

2. Read a Book – Again, typically an easy task to achieve; doesn't even have to be a long book. There are a lot of great books on leadership, management, team-building, staff development, etc. Pick one

book a month and really read it, meaning grab a highlighter and approach it with intentional learning. A few suggestions are: "Grit," "7 Habits of Highly Effective People," "Drive," and "Extreme Ownership."

Start by increasing your own supply, then you can continue to pour out to your staff and development doesn't become stagnant.

bject: CPR Report

Free Space to write down key takeaways or answers to any questions found in this week's email:

_____

_____

_____

_____

Questions

Answer any challenging questions the email posed to you:

_____

_____

_____

_____

Challenge

What was the leadership challenge that spoke to you this week?

_____

_____

_____

_____

Perform

How do you plan to perform the challenges this week?

_____

_____

_____

_____

Repetitions

What do you need to do to remind yourself to get your reps in this week?

_____

_____

_____

_____

CPR Progress Report

(1 Needed Major Improvement - 5 CRUSHED IT!)

Rate yourself 1-5 on your leadership challenge this week

1   2   3   4   5

Rate 1-5 how well do you think you performed this week

1   2   3   4   5

Rate 1-5 how often you feel like you were consistent with your reps this week

1   2   3   4   5

Mine is slowly starting to fill up. I have never really been a *Tim the Tool* man handyman. I'm more like, who can I call to do this quicker and better than I can?

I think it's because I lack the patience to really appreciate the process of building. As I have gotten older, I have begun to get a little more interested in the whole DIY movement. I am also not too ashamed to admit that Faith is actually really good at house projects. Remember the whole patience thing we talked about? That's right up her lane.

I was talking with a coach about the art and skills of coaching and how you can relate that to any other job. In the process, I found out I have been a carpenter all along. The main difference is, I wasn't building houses; I was building people. This doesn't just have to be a coach. I strongly believe these four principles cross over into management, sales, and other professions.

I want you to take a second and write each of the principles of coaching out. Then write down three ways you have used these in the past week with your team. If nothing comes right to the top of your mind, then skip that one. Then what I want you to is find out where your gaps are. Then fill in those gaps with one need in each category.

Four Principles of a Carpenter Coach/Leader:

Coaching with Empathy:

Great coaches know that to become great, you first must be able to relate. There is only one way to relate and it's by doing. There have been moments I am sure you have had to give out some verbal hugs because you saw the need to be empathetic. That's because you can relate with what they are experiencing. Being able to relate is like the hammer of a coach's tool belt. There is part of that tool that can drive a nail into the post, then there is part of the hammer that can pull that nail back if needed. Empathy is the ability to see where you can drive (push) a little more, but also where you may need to pull back.

Coaching with Corrections:

As a coach, I know this is probably one of the most frustrating ones. It's like you just said: Shoulders back, chest up, and the minute you turn around, the shoulders fall and it's like they didn't even listen. What I will tell you is it's not just members who need constant corrections. Think of the corrections like your measuring tape. When building anything, I know I always end up measuring a few times before I cut. As a coach, corrections are just making sure that you have measured and double-checked your work. You may have to correct someone two to three times. That's okay. I know I have measured the piece of wood at least twice and where that wood is going two to three times, especially if you are down to the last couple of cuts. This is a great tool because once you have measured and corrected, it allows for a precision of execution.

Coaching with Challenges:

Have you ever used a nail gun? Man, they are fun. Guess what, they are also scary when used incorrectly. Kind of like challenges; they are really fun to give and see a member complete if capable. They can also be scary if that member isn't quite ready for that specific challenge. There is an art to the challenge. You have to know where your "studs" are before you can shoot; and to do that, you need to measure. Everyone goes through a season of challenge. You have to be able to identify where they are in their seasons. Are they ripe for the challenge or do you need to take a moment and get your hammer back out? Because when you use that nail gun, it's not as easy to get that nail out. Usually, it will cause some extra damage or extra time. Know when and where you can challenge; just like when and where to shoot the gun, into the stud after you have measured.

Coaching with Congratulations:

This is your wood putty. Do you really need it? I mean is anyone really going to look that closely? Yes, they will. To have a finished product, you need wood putty. The purpose of the wood putty is to fill the punctures. Think about this for a second. Do you ever congratulate someone who hasn't experienced some sort of pain or discomfort? I didn't say that's the only time, but think about it. Graduation, for example; I am sure there was a moment where that person experienced some sort of pain or discomfort in their schooling. Congratulations are meant to be celebratory after someone has accomplished something that requires effort. When building something, you fill in the holes of your effort to smooth the final product out. You have learned how to congratulate people after they have accomplished feats they never thought possible. Everyone's abilities are different and knowing that will allow you to use the correct amount of wood putty to fill in the puncture.

Think about a coach who leads people. This doesn't apply to just coaching people during exercise. You can apply these tools to anyone you are coaching.

What tools are missing from your belt?

What tools do you need to get back out and use?

Subject: CPR Report

Free Space to write down key takeaways or answers to any questions found in this week's email:

_____

_____

_____

_____

Questions

Answer any challenging questions the email posed to you:

_____

_____

_____

_____

Challenge

What was the leadership challenge that spoke to you this week?

_____

_____

_____

_____

Perform

How do you plan to perform the challenges this week?

_____

_____

_____

_____

Repetitions

What do you need to do to remind yourself to get your reps in this week?

_____

_____

_____

_____

CPR Progress Report

(1 Needed Major Improvement - 5 CRUSHED IT!)

Rate yourself 1-5 on your leadership challenge this week

1   2   3   4   5

Rate 1-5 how well do you think you performed this week

1   2   3   4   5

Rate 1-5 how often you feel like you were consistent with your reps this week

1   2   3   4   5

Subject: **Triple A Treatment**

- Attention
- Affirmation
- Appreciation

Focusing on the three actions shown above will help you focus on the value of the person you are talking to, and avoid being self-absorbed. These actions are great ways to engage members in the lobby before class, while creating relationships. This works with anyone you meet, but in our world of OTF, we have members and coaches. There are a few examples below describing how to use the actions with members and coaches.

Attention:

- Member Example: Draw attention to an achievement you know has happened recently in that person's life. This applies to members and coaches alike. This is a great way to start the first thirty seconds of a convo with a member. Remember, it's about bringing attention to *them*.

- Coach Example: A coach who taught a great class, passed their cert, graduated from school, or any small or big achievement needs attention drawn to them.

Affirmation

- Member Example: Emotional support or encouragement for members. After you have brought attention to them, the next step is to offer some encouraging words and support.

- Coach Example: Let them know what they did really well and encourage them to keep up with that one great thing.

Appreciation

- Member Example: The last thirty seconds of a conversation shows appreciation. You can appreciate the members for coming to your class, working hard today after class is over, or for just being a rock star member.

- Coach Example: Thank them for always showing up on time for classes or for always being prepared for class. Maybe they taught X number of classes, taking great care of the members, and always provides the OTF experience.

Try and remember these three words next time we engage with others. If you follow the TOP SECRET RULE, you will have better engagement from those you are talking to and, in turn, create better relationships.

Subject: CPR Report

Free Space to write down key takeaways or answers to any questions found in this week's email:

_____

_____

_____

_____

Questions

Answer any challenging questions the email posed to you:

_____

_____

_____

_____

Challenge

What was the leadership challenge that spoke to you this week?

_____

_____

_____

_____

Perform

How do you plan to perform the challenges this week?

_____

_____

_____

_____

Repetitions

What do you need to do to remind yourself to get your reps in this week?

_____

_____

_____

_____

CPR Progress Report

(1 Needed Major Improvement - 5 CRUSHED IT!)

Rate yourself 1-5 on your leadership challenge this week

1   2   3   4   5

Rate 1-5 how well do you think you performed this week

1   2   3   4   5

Rate 1-5 how often you feel like you were consistent with your reps this week

1   2   3   4   5

Subject: The New 3-Cs

This is not what you may assume: The *Correct, Challenge, and Congratulate* coaching method is still how we approach our members while in class and, really, anytime. But I am talking about the 3-Cs of a *coach*.

We talk a lot about finding the perfect coach, the one who will save the day. Speaking of saving the day, we can draw a comparison between the perfect coach and superheroes. As we all know (I hope), Marvel movies are fictional. While Ironman and Thor are superheroes, they only exist in the Marvel Cinematic Universe. Each one has some commonalities. Superheroes typically wear some type of uniform. This is how you can identify them when they are in superhero mode. Next, most heroes have secret identities. Clark Kent as Superman, Bruce Wayne as Batman, and Bruce Banner as the Hulk. Lastly, you can't say superhero without talking about their superpowers. These are identifying qualities each of these superheroes would have on their resumes. I believe the 3-Cs below is a recipe for modeling a superhero coach.

I am calling these the *3-Cs to Superhero Coaching*.

The First C stands for compassion. Compassion is the uniform of coaching. Every good superhero needs a uniform. Think about it; why do coaches get into the industry? If you ask a coach, most will say it was to change someone's life. You can't have passion without *compassion*. Why do people coach sports teams? They are passionate about that sport but ultimately compassionate about helping athletes perform better. Passion is the gateway to compassion. Passion is what you love; compassion is what keeps you *in love*.

How do you know if your coaches have compassion?

- Do they take class? It's really hard to be a good coach if you don't understand the product you are coaching. If you don't know what a three-minute push feels like, you can't coach it properly.

- Does your coach have a member-first approach? Our members walk in our doors with problems you could probably never imagine; some big, some small, but all are problems just the same. When they walk in our doors, that one hour should be all about them and their experience, not you.

- Do they encourage others? Not just when a member hits a PR. Do they genuinely encourage members, no matter how big or small their achievements? Think, for some people, just showing up is a PR!

- Are they humble? Being humble is simply knowing that you are no better than anyone else. We all have struggles and to truly be compassionate, I believe being humble helps achieve it.

Since compassion is the uniform of coaching, then confidence is the identity. Superheroes usually have an alter-ego or a secret identity. It's important that superheroes have a secret identity. If Clark Kent never went in the phone booth and change his uniform and his identity, would the individuals he is trying to save have the certainty he could complete the job? If the identity didn't change, the level of certainty wouldn't either.

One of the basic human needs is *certainty*; people like certainty. If you buy a brand-new car, you have the confidence that it won't break down the minute you drive it off the lot. With confidence comes certainty.

How do you know if your coaches have confidence?

- Do they believe in the product? If your coaches don't take classes and believe in the product, then there is no way they can deliver that message to your members.

- Do they always do the right thing? Confidence is knowing that doing the right thing sometimes may cause someone to look weak, when, in reality, it doesn't matter what others think when you are doing the right thing.

- Do they fall and get back up? There is the old saying, *fall seven times, stand up eight*. It's okay to fall or fail as long as that doesn't define you. What defines you is your ability to try, try again until you succeed.

We have all the elements of a superhero, minus the most important part—the superpower. This is where *charisma* comes in; this is the true super-power of a coach, the compelling attractiveness and charm that can inspire devotion in others. Man, that is a power definition that should make all of you sit up a little taller and want that power!

How do you tell if your coaches have *charisma*?

- Do they help others feel confident? Being in a position to boost someone's confidence is such a powerful tool. When you can help someone become more confident, you can truly change his or her life. Having charisma gives you the ability to do this.

- Do your coaches care? Or are your coaches just showing up to read a template? Or do they truly love their jobs? Caring is what most of our members are searching for. They just want someone to listen and care about them. They have to have the ability to motivate and relate.

- Do they show commitment? People who have charisma believe in something so powerfully that it, in turn, attracts others to want to be a part of it. Are they committed to the brand, the mission, vision, and values? Are they committed to their members? Are they committed to the team? Are they committed to you as the head coach? Lastly, are they committed to the never-ending pursuit of growing their skills?

Everyone, we need to take a serious look at our coaches and find those superheroes that do exist. We are facing an enemy (our competitors) who wants nothing more than to give a better experience to your members. So, assemble your avengers and let's *win* this battle.

Subject: **CPR Report**

Free Space to write down key takeaways or answers to any questions found in this week's email:

_____

_____

_____

_____

Questions

Answer any challenging questions the email posed to you:

_____

_____

_____

_____

Challenge

What was the leadership challenge that spoke to you this week?

_____

_____

_____

_____

Perform

How do you plan to perform the challenges this week?

_____

_____

_____

_____

Repetitions

What do you need to do to remind yourself to get your reps in this week?

_____

_____

_____

_____

CPR Progress Report

(1 Needed Major Improvement - 5 CRUSHED IT!)

Rate yourself 1-5 on your leadership challenge this week

1   2   3   4   5

Rate 1-5 how well do you think you performed this week

1   2   3   4   5

Rate 1-5 how often you feel like you were consistent with your reps this week

1   2   3   4   5

Subject: ABC

I know what you are thinking... another email? Yes! However, today we are unpacking some deeper content from yesterday. Not only will this make you a better coach, it will help you grow your classes and make bigger impacts on the members in front of you each day; ultimately helping them achieve whatever problem they came to us with.

As we talked about making coaching a service business, I gave you three qualities that could help you change your mindset. It's really easy. I believe we start with the ABCs of Building Community. You have heard the saying, "Your vibe is your tribe." If you haven't then, that's a bonus takeaway.

So many times I've talked to coaches and business owners around the network, and there remains one constant that divides success and those who are struggling.

Community of your customers: There are a lot of brands that build customer loyalty through many different avenues. I believe in the fitness industry we have to do things a little differently. Below are my ABCs of building a bulletproof community.

Bulletproof Community:

Acknowledge

- Everyone wants to be noticed, especially in the fast-paced society we live in today. People can easily be left behind or overlooked while others around them dash about.

- Acknowledgment is as simple as making eye contact with a member from across the room. It lets them know you see them and you have their back.

- Use their names with genuine care. Saying a name to check it off the box doesn't cut it when it comes to building a bulletproof community.

Blessing

- If you are trying to impress someone, you can't bless them. So instead of trying to be impressive, be a blessing.

- You never know what's going on in someone's day or life. Until you create a relationship with your members, you can't bless them through your interactions.

- Blessing are small. It could be a little note left for them that you are thinking about them in their situation. An extra pat on the back during their workout. A *thank-you* email for coming to your class today, even though you know their kids are sick and they are super busy. Remember, they are paying your bills.

Celebrate

- I know we celebrate PR's… how about the small victories like the first push-up, first time running the whole class, ten classes achieved, or even twenty-five classes. Remember, most of our members are not "fitness freaks." Working out ten times is a big accomplishment for some of them.

- Celebrate your members on social media, bragging on your members a little; it makes them feel good.

- Tell their stories of how they got to their celebration moments. If it's a PR, then talk about where they started and how far they've come.

- Give out little awards during class. If it's a benchmark day, have your studio print up certificates for top three and award them with their certifications.

Over the next few days, try to take these ABCs with you inside the glass walls of the studio.

bject: CPR Report

Free Space to write down key takeaways or answers to any questions found in this week's email:

_____

_____

_____

_____

Questions

Answer any challenging questions the email posed to you:

_____

_____

_____

_____

Challenge

What was the leadership challenge that spoke to you this week?

_____

_____

_____

_____

Perform

How do you plan to perform the challenges this week?

_____

_____

_____

_____

Repetitions

What do you need to do to remind yourself to get your reps in this week?

_____

_____

_____

_____

CPR Progress Report

(1 Needed Major Improvement - 5 CRUSHED IT!)

Rate yourself 1-5 on your leadership challenge this week

1   2   3   4   5

Rate 1-5 how well do you think you performed this week

1   2   3   4   5

Rate 1-5 how often you feel like you were consistent with your reps this week

1   2   3   4   5

bject: Do You Have an Edge?

Before you answer that, I should probably define which
type of edge I'm talking about.

There are two different types of edges.

First, you can *be* on edge. This is where you are in a
precarious situation and you are in a heightened state of
excitement due to possible danger or risk.

Or, you can *have* an edge. This is where you have an
advantage or you are in the proper position to be more
successful.

Think for a second; which side of the edge have
you been on?

As leaders, I don't think either edge is a bad thing. "Okay,
Heath, so you are telling me it's ok to be in danger? That
doesn't sound like a good leader." This is not the type
of danger or risk like me asking you to drive a car with
no brakes.

I know this might be confusing; leadership is not black and
white; It's malleable. We need to be able to reshape as
needed without breaking. Okay, we should probably save
malleable leadership for another week.

Let's get back to the EDGE.

To be on edge is good; this means you have taken a risk; a
risk that you actually care about the outcome. See, being
on edge means you have an investment in that situation.

Point number 1:

Be invested in your risk-taking. I'll give you a prime example of not being invested in a risk. This happened to me last week.

My next-door neighbor's ten-year-old daughter was selling raffle tickets for her softball team. There were three different prizes. Each ticket cost $10. I'll be completely honest, I think I threw the ticket away. It's not a risk I really cared about. It was a good cause helping out a neighbor, and her mom used to be a member and will be again in the future. I know the probability of winning is low, so I only bought one ticket, which is why the investment level isn't there. Now, if I would have bought a hundred tickets, that's a much different story.

Point number 2:

If you don't invest, neither will your team. As leaders, when we take a risk, it should stir up investment in our teams as well. Think about Dri-Tri. Our members took a risk. They paid $25 for an event they didn't even know if they could complete. While they were on edge about competing, our teams were totally invested in making sure they completed Dri-Tri. When the team is unified and invested in the success of the risk, we are only positioning ourselves for better teamwork and shared success at the outcome.

Being on edge isn't a bad thing. Now, if you are addicted to the lottery and spent your rent money in hopes of hitting the Powerball, then, that may be a risk you want to reconsider.

Having an edge is like hitting the Powerball lottery.

This is like having the cheat codes for your favorite game.

Having an edge gives you swagger. You play the game differently when you have the codes. You become a little more confident and maybe play with a higher level of excitement.

Point number 1:

When you have an edge, you have more confidence. Think about those members who have done Dri-Tri before. They came in with a little bit of swagger; they had an edge about them. They knew where to conserve and when to push, unlike the newbies who were just hoping for survival.

As a leader, having an edge is about knowing the next three steps. It's not always about *experience*; it's about members and the game plan. How many of your coaches were giving out strategy yesterday to members? One of our coaches didn't have a ton of experience coaching the treadmill for Dri-Tri. I noticed two quick areas I could help him. I gave him two quick tips how to coach the treads a little differently. I noticed an increased confidence with just those two quick tips. Confidence will boost your edge. If you know just a little bit more than the person next to you, that little bit is your edge.

Point number 2:

Pass the edge on. As a leader, if you have an edge somewhere, pass it on. Don't keep it for yourself and be greedy. If you beat King Koopa, help a brother out. Give me some tips. Your team will not only have more confidence to perform better, they will have a level of trust in you that opens the door for you to climb the influential leadership ladder.

I want to challenge each of you this week to take a risk that causes you to be on edge.

The second challenge is to pass on some swagger to a teammate this week. Give someone else an edge.

Have a great week, everyone!

bject: CPR Report

Free Space to write down key takeaways or answers to any questions found in this week's email:

_____

_____

_____

_____

Questions

Answer any challenging questions the email posed to you:

_____

_____

_____

_____

Challenge

What was the leadership challenge that spoke to you this week?

_____

_____

_____

_____

Perform

How do you plan to perform the challenges this week?

_____

_____

_____

_____

Repetitions

What do you need to do to remind yourself to get your reps in this week?

_____

_____

_____

_____

CPR Progress Report

(1 Needed Major Improvement - 5 CRUSHED IT!)

Rate yourself 1-5 on your leadership challenge this week

1   2   3   4   5

Rate 1-5 how well do you think you performed this week

1   2   3   4   5

Rate 1-5 how often you feel like you were consistent with your reps this week

1   2   3   4   5

bject: Do You Have an Owner's Mindset?

But Heath, I'm not an owner, just a manager. So what you are telling me is you don't care about the business as much as the owner does?

Probably not a good first interview answer.

I know people say no one will love the business like the owner does. Well, I am here to tell you that is false. We have people on our team right now that you couldn't tell they weren't owners. They treat this business as if it was theirs.

Don't get me wrong; that statement holds true for a lot of people. Why though? Well, I think it's because no one loves the business for the same reasons you opened. Also, they have no risk in the success of the business. If it fails, most employees will find other jobs.

If you have ever struggled with having that *owner mindset*, you probably haven't found the right place for you. How do you know if it's the right place?

The following statements are how you know if you are in the right place or not. These will help position you for an owner mindset. You never care about the extra hours you put in. You don't do it for the pay. You know you are making a difference. There is so much to lose but even more to gain.

I want everyone to have an owner mindset. It doesn't matter what position you hold in the company.

I want to give you three quick takeaways on how to align yourself with your company and adapt the owner mindset.

Love the VALUES

Every company has values; they are the company's core.
It's what stabilizes them.

I believe every studio should have values. Those values
should be in line with the company values. Values are so
important to companies. I have heard there are companies
that share their values with a candidate in the first
interview. Then ask if the candidate's values align with the
companies. If a personal value of yours isn't integrity and
the company's is, then you're never going to align properly.

If you don't love the values, you will never have an
owner mindset.

Live the MISSION

A company mission kind of acts as the day-to-day checklist
of how to achieve the overall company vision. The mission
speaks to what we do as a company, how we do it, and
why we do it. Every day, when you show up to work, you
are living the mission of that business. You have to be 100
percent bought into the mission of your business.

If you don't believe in what you do or why you do it, your
motivation will never align with the initiatives the company
is trying to achieve.

Loyal to the VISION

A company's vision is typically a long-term view of what they
would like to accomplish, like living the mission daily. You
have to be loyal to the long-term goals of the company.

When I think of loyalty, I think of commitments like
marriage. If your marriage is aligned with loyalty, then you

have confidence that your partner is faithful to the vows you each took. The vision is usually where the business is birthed. If you're not loyal to the cause, you will never align with an owner mindset.

To put it simply:

The vision is why you are there.

The mission is what you show up to do.

The values are how you act when you show up.

Ask yourself what you need to do to align yourself with these goals to create that owner mindset.

Subject: CPR Report

Free Space to write down key takeaways or answers to any questions found in this week's email:

_____

_____

_____

_____

Questions

Answer any challenging questions the email posed to you:

_____

_____

_____

_____

Challenge

What was the leadership challenge that spoke to you this week?

_____

_____

_____

_____

Perform

How do you plan to perform the challenges this week?

_____

_____

_____

_____

Repetitions

What do you need to do to remind yourself to get your reps in this week?

_____

_____

_____

_____

CPR Progress Report

(1 Needed Major Improvement - 5 CRUSHED IT!)

Rate yourself 1-5 on your leadership challenge this week

1   2   3   4   5

Rate 1-5 how well do you think you performed this week

1   2   3   4   5

Rate 1-5 how often you feel like you were consistent with your reps this week

1   2   3   4   5

Subject: Leadership WOP

This is not a song you will hear Cardi B. singing. This isn't a popular line dance.

This is such a simple acronym for you to remember. Keep it in your mind so you can access it on a daily basis.

In the workplace, people are constantly looking for affirmation. Why?

Because they want to know they are doing a good job. It's unfortunate that most employees don't know they are doing a good job until the end-of-year awards ceremony. You know, the events they probably don't even want to go to because they think no one notices them.

But you go because, if not, you'll be the topic of conversation at the Monday morning coffee-gossip hour.

You get there and enjoy a nice dinner, which you think, *Well, I deserve this for all the hard unnoticed work I do.* The extra thirty minutes I give here or there, the Friday night crisis phone call, or how about when that co-worker was late and you stayed extra.

Once dinner is over, the awards start. You sit back in your chair and grab your cellphone to start scrolling for a new outfit—until you hear your name over the loudspeakers.

You look up and all eyes are on you. You set your phone down and, as you walk toward the stage, you are trying to guess what award you could possibly be getting. No one ever says *great job* or *thank you.* You actually signed up for an Indeed account and started looking for other job options.

As you climb on stage, you are presented with the summit award. It's the award that represents the person who has climbed to the top, overcome obstacles, and outperformed the rest.

To say you are shocked is an understatement. You smile and accept your award. You hear your boss, for the first time, say, *"Great job, we are lucky to have you!"*

Really? You don't know whether to be excited or furious.

Has this ever happened to you or someone you know? Maybe on a slightly smaller scale.

This type of recognition goes two ways.

First, you never hear anything because you are either meeting the expectation of the job, or you are completely bombing, and that's the only time you hear from your boss.

Why wait?

That's where Leadership WOP comes into play.

Think of this as a game with Words of Praise.

Think of thirty-one different words or phrases of praise.

Write or print them on individual pieces of paper.

Over the next month, hand them out as you see fit. When you hand one to your employees, let them know why they are receiving that specific one. The goal is to collect them all, like Pokémon!

Have fun and make Leadership WOP a daily habit.

Subject: CPR Report

Free Space to write down key takeaways or answers to any questions found in this week's email:

_____

_____

_____

_____

Questions

Answer any challenging questions the email posed to you:

_____

_____

_____

_____

Challenge

What was the leadership challenge that spoke to you this week?

_____

_____

_____

_____

Perform

How do you plan to perform the challenges this week?

_____

_____

_____

_____

Repetitions

What do you need to do to remind yourself to get your reps in this week?

_____

_____

_____

_____

CPR Progress Report

(1 Needed Major Improvement - 5 CRUSHED IT!)

Rate yourself 1-5 on your leadership challenge this week

1   2   3   4   5

Rate 1-5 how well do you think you performed this week

1   2   3   4   5

Rate 1-5 how often you feel like you were consistent with your reps this week

1   2   3   4   5

Subject: Don't Worry

It's not something you need to drive to the ER for. However, it is a real symptom, especially now with social media and how quickly we want things to happen. If you have ever had a case of FOMO, you know how it kind of consumes your thoughts, and most likely your wallets.

What is FOMO?

For those of you who don't know, it's the Fear of Missing Out, which is a play on emotions and thoughts.

In our first week of Redefining Fitness, I want to take a minute and give you some FOMO; as well as some ideas on how to use FOMO to keep your customers coming back to take classes and not cancel.

Just be careful. If you use these tactics, you may have to keep some Xanax on hand for all the anxiety you will be causing. You'll also need to open a savings account for all the extra money you will be stashing.

Create a "HIGH DEMAND" environment

- We do this very well during Pre-Sales—with our limited tier prices. It's a high-demand environment for those special tier one and two memberships. These are in high demand because they are limited. There are many different types businesses that create "Limited" type offering. You create H.D. when supply is low and demand is high. What can you offer a short supply of and create high demand for? This could be anything, limited amount of a special piece of retail. Putting a special class on the schedule once a month instead of having it once a week. The concept of High Demand is simple. The execution is the piece you really need to nail down.

Create an Exclusive Environment

- Everyone wants to feel like they are exclusive. Who in our business is exclusive? The founders. When was the last time you did something special for just them? Or when did you give them a reason to be proud of being a founding member? Make them feel like they are special. Because they are; they help you build your studio. How do you do this? You could do a special class just for founder and cater a lunch or happy hour after. Create a Special T-Shirt or water bottle for them. One of our managers send a card in the mail thanking them personally and wrote really big how many lifetime classes they had taken. This is a very nice touch. Hotels do this very well the more nights you stay, the more exclusive benefits you get.

Create a Competitive Environment

- *Competition doesn't have to be related to winning a sporting event. I was just thinking about when Disney launches a new ride. It's a competition to get in line first when the park opens. Or be one of the first ones to book a fast pass before they are all gone. Think about this all your friends rode the new ride. They are all talking about how awesome it was, you begin to feel left out. So next time you are going to make sure you are first in line. That's the FOMO affect. Maybe you are more of a concert person. Think about a concert you missed and people you know went and all the talked about for 2 days was how amazing it was. You are going to make sure next time you don't miss out.* New attractions create a competitive environment and will leave people with FOMO is they don't compete for a spot.

As we wrap this email up this week. I want you to think about the last time you went Black Friday shopping. There are only ten TV's for a super low price. This can be replaced with whatever product you want. Black Friday is leaving people with FOMO every year. I have seen like many of you the fights that happen on Black Friday everywhere because people missed out. That's FOMO to the next level. When was the last time you had people fighting each other to get to your business or classes?

Ask you team this week these 3 questions:

What do we have that we can create High Demand for?

How can we better serve our loyal members and show we apricate them?

How can we create a new attraction that members are going to go nuts over?

bject: CPR Report

Free Space to write down key takeaways or answers to any questions found in this week's email:

_____

_____

_____

_____

Questions

Answer any challenging questions the email posed to you:

_____

_____

_____

_____

Challenge

What was the leadership challenge that spoke to you this week?

_____

_____

_____

_____

Perform

How do you plan to perform the challenges this week?

_____

_____

_____

_____

Repetitions

What do you need to do to remind yourself to get your reps in this week?

_____

_____

_____

_____

CPR Progress Report

(1 Needed Major Improvement - 5 CRUSHED IT!)

Rate yourself 1-5 on your leadership challenge this week

1   2   3   4   5

Rate 1-5 how well do you think you performed this week

1   2   3   4   5

Rate 1-5 how often you feel like you were consistent with your reps this week

1   2   3   4   5

bject: **Are You Suffering?**

If not, you should be. You read that right. If you aren't suffering, then you are lacking passion. I met with a mentor of mine this past week, and we talked about passion and how the true meaning of passion is suffering.

Probably not a word you would associate with the word *passion*, but it's so true if you actually think about it.

In week two of our Redefining Fitness series, we are going to explore three questions to find out if you are suffering from what 87 percent of the US workforce suffers from— lack of passion.

Before I ask you these questions, let's see how lack of passion can actually cause suffering.

- Are your classes suffering?

  - Are you only looking at the class tomorrow that has a wait-list? How about looking at that same class next week or two weeks from now? Pre-book your members for those classes.

- Is your studio suffering?

  - Lack of leads? Are your SAs passionately seeking new leads? Lack of sales? Are your SAs upset when they don't close a sale? Member Mix out of whack? Are your SAs and coaches setting the member up for success?

- Is your staff suffering?

  - Lack of growth? Are you passionate about development? Staff being lazy? Is that because you just task them instead of teach them *the why?* Not coaching better classes? Are your coaches taking enough OTF classes?

- Are your members suffering?

  - No results? Do your coaches take the time to actually connect? Are we taking the time to become better at our craft? Are members canceling memberships? Are they being forgotten about? Do you actually care?

I believe if you can answer yes to any of the questions above... insert passion.

You are probably highly confused right now... don't worry; it will all make sense.

Passion is hardly being able to control your emotions toward your purpose.

Suffering is a state of distress or hardship.

We can turn away from our sufferings and cure them with passion. But not everyone has found their passion and many have forgotten theirs.

Find or re-ignite your passion by answering these three questions:

- What your feeds your soul daily?

  - What do you do that you can totally lose yourself in?

- If money wasn't an object, what would you do?

  - Think about a time in your life you have done this. What was it and how did you feel?

- What skills come naturally to you?

  - How could you use those skills to make a living?

Find your passion, and you and your business will stop suffering.

Have a great week, everyone!

Subject: **CPR Report**

Free Space to write down key takeaways or answers to any questions found in this week's email:

_____

_____

_____

_____

Questions

Answer any challenging questions the email posed to you:

_____

_____

_____

_____

Challenge

What was the leadership challenge that spoke to you this week?

_____

_____

_____

_____

Perform

How do you plan to perform the challenges this week?

_____

_____

_____

_____

Repetitions

What do you need to do to remind yourself to get your reps in this week?

_____

_____

_____

_____

CPR Progress Report

(1 Needed Major Improvement - 5 CRUSHED IT!)

Rate yourself 1-5 on your leadership challenge this week

1   2   3   4   5

Rate 1-5 how well do you think you performed this week

1   2   3   4   5

Rate 1-5 how often you feel like you were consistent with your reps this week

1   2   3   4   5

Subject: I Just Have to "Get Through" it

STOP!

Too many times I've heard, "I have to just *get through* it!" I just have to "*get through*" the end of the year; I just have to "*get through*" this last class; I just have to "*get through*" this week; I just have to "*get through*" training these new sales associates.

STOP AND THINK ABOUT THIS.

If you are taking this attitude with you through your class, your year, your training, your week,

then yeah, I bet you can't wait to "*get through*" it.

Congratulations. You made it through.

STOP. I HAVE A QUESTION FOR YOU.

Are you working for the #1 fitness company in the world so you can just "*get through*" it? Do you know what a "*get through*" it mindset is? It's an epidemic that will spread throughout your business, your relationships, and your life. Especially being in a position of leadership, you cannot have a "*get through it*" mindset. Your job is to inspire, not discourage. To inspire literally means: to encourage somebody to greater effort, enthusiasm, or creativity.

STOP AND REALLY THINK ABOUT THIS.

WHAT DID YOU GET OUT OF IT?

Let's break this down.

Answer these five questions below on what you get out of it. (It can be whatever it is you are just trying to *"get through."*)

- What do I get out of it personally?

- What do I get out of it financially?

- What do I get out of it professionally?

- What do I get out of it emotionally?

- What do I get out of it positively?

Once you can answer those five questions on what you get out of it, I believe you will find that you aren't just trying to *"get through"* it! If you are, that's okay; we have all said it at one point. But maybe this exercise will bring back some perspective as to why you do it.

Subject: CPR Report

Free Space to write down key takeaways or answers to any questions found in this week's email:

_____

_____

_____

_____

Questions

Answer any challenging questions the email posed to you:

_____

_____

_____

_____

Challenge

What was the leadership challenge that spoke to you this week?

_____

_____

_____

_____

Perform

How do you plan to perform the challenges this week?

_____

_____

_____

_____

Repetitions

What do you need to do to remind yourself to get your reps in this week?

_____

_____

_____

_____

CPR Progress Report

(1 Needed Major Improvement - 5 CRUSHED IT!)

Rate yourself 1-5 on your leadership challenge this week

1   2   3   4   5

Rate 1-5 how well do you think you performed this week

1   2   3   4   5

Rate 1-5 how often you feel like you were consistent with your reps this week

1   2   3   4   5

Subject: **Ethos**

Ethos is a Greek word meaning *character* that is used to describe the guiding beliefs or ideals that characterize a community.

Every great team has an ethos they operate by.

The Navy Seals have an ethos from day one that their recruits are expected to know, respect, and uphold. Even though we are not out there generating wins for America, we are helping our members win.

Do you have an ethos for your team? What we have decided to do is create leadership principles we all operate by. We did a great team building activity, every manager and assistant manager had the opportunity to help create our leadership principles.

There were two leaders to a page a paper, they were challenged to come up with a leadership principle and write it down. Then the fun part. They had to role play to the group how that principle would play out in real time. Not only did everyone have fun with this activity. It also allowed everyone to have a voice in creating the principles we operate in daily.

Here are our Leadership Principles for an example:

- Lead by Example
- Limited Short-Term Memory
- Be a product of your product
- No ZERO days
- Ownership pf responsibilities

- Be an empathetic problem solver

- Effective Expression

- Be masterly

- Consistent customer satisfaction

- Committing to the product instead of problems

If you want to create epic teams that not only change the game but leave a legacy, I believe you must follow in the footsteps of those teams and organizations that have already done that.

I want to leave you with a small piece of the Navy Seal Creed that I think should speak to every single one of us.

"We expect to lead and be led. In the absence of orders, I will take charge, lead my teammates and accomplish the mission. I lead by example in all situations."

What is your ethos or leadership principles?

Subject: CPR Report

Free Space to write down key takeaways or answers to any questions found in this week's email:

_____

_____

_____

_____

Questions

Answer any challenging questions the email posed to you:

_____

_____

_____

Challenge

What was the leadership challenge that spoke to you this week?

_____

_____

_____

_____

Perform

How do you plan to perform the challenges this week?

_____

_____

_____

_____

Repetitions

What do you need to do to remind yourself to get your reps in this week?

_____

_____

_____

_____

CPR Progress Report

(1 Needed Major Improvement - 5 CRUSHED IT!)

Rate yourself 1-5 on your leadership challenge this week

1   2   3   4   5

Rate 1-5 how well do you think you performed this week

1   2   3   4   5

Rate 1-5 how often you feel like you were consistent with your reps this week

1   2   3   4   5

Subject: **Prepare Brew**

Pre-workouts date back to the late eighties or early nineties with Ultimate Orange. The fitness enthusiast is no stranger to the artificial taste of blue-raspberry pre-workout juice. After about fifteen minutes, your skin begins to tingle a little, your core temperature rises, and you start to feel your heart-beat in your ears. This is when you know your pre has "kicked in."

Now that your internal fuse has been lit by the ingredients of the blue-raspberry juice, you are primed and ready to endure another session of pumping muscle up, while simultaneously tearing them down.

The first couple of reps begin to flood your system with the proper nutrients your muscles need to recover faster and fill a little fuller. For the next hour, you seem unstoppable, your physique changes form, and you begin to experience Spidey Vision. Then it happens, as quickly as it hits your system, the pre-workout leaves you tired, deflated, and wishing you could keep that false sense of pump and energy all day.

I believe sometimes, as leaders, we tend to be one scoop short for our teams. Leaders and coaches are like that pre-workout powder:

- Starts off with a bang
- Pumps your body up
- Elevates your enthusiasm

Usually, as quickly as those feelings come on, they leave just as quickly. We need staying power. Imagine an IV drip. The IV will slowly drip into your system, continually supplying your body with the proper amount of what it needs. So how can leaders craft the right pre-workout formula?

In this three-part email series, we are going to explore three different proprietary blends in the leaders' pre-workout mix.

What is a proprietary blend, you ask?

If you can think of a supplement label, usually there will be certain ingredients in blended formulas on the back. Example, it might be Extreme Energy Blend, Nitric Rush Mix, Creatine Concoction. Then under each blend, they would have their ingredients listed that would help achieve the desired results.

I would like you to picture that label. We are going to have three proprietary blends in our mixture.

As leaders and coaches, we need to prepare our heads and hearts for all situations and scenarios. There are three key ingredients in our prepare brew that will make sure you are able to see, listen, and feel at different altitudes.

Prepare Brew- (How you prepare yourself)

Posture -I'm not talking about slouching your shoulders forward and making sure you can balance a book on top of your head. Nah. The posture I'm talking about is how you position yourself to start your week. Being a manager or holding a title in a business means nothing if there is an absence of a leadership posture. A leader's posture is how you carry yourself in all situations; your attitude no matter the circumstance. Lastly, your ability to stay poised under pressure. Lou Holtz said, "It's not the load that breaks you it's how you carry it." Posture yourself so you can carry the load this week. If you get to Wednesday and you didn't posture yourself correctly on Sunday, then you will feel the weight of that load begin to take its toll.

Priorities- You all hear me talk about priorities so often. Once you have the proper posture, you next need to get your priorities in line. Steven Covey said, "The key is not to prioritize what's on your schedule but to schedule your priorities." This is why every Sunday, when I send out the weekly manager outlook email, I always talk about your first thirty minutes. Those are your scheduled priorities this way after the first thirty minutes of your day. You can get caught in the whirlwind and it doesn't pull you off track. Plus, if you finish your first thirty-minute priority list, you will have a small *win* to start the day. If you have your priorities in line, then you will be able to provide better focus for your teams.

Punctuality- You can't start your first thirty minutes on time, then your whole day will be thrown off. Being punctual doesn't mean just showing up on time to a meeting or a shift. It's much more than that. It sets an example for your team. It's hard to have a conversation with a team member about being tardy if you can't show up on time. You set the tone for your team by being punctual in all aspects. I want to give you three specific topics to be punctual with.

- Be punctual with your communication. Your team needs to know what's coming. Your GPS always gives you plenty of notice before you have to make a turn.

Be punctual with feedback. When you see an opportunity to provide feedback, make sure you are punctual. Overdue feedback is worthless; it doesn't help anyone.

- Be punctual with daily expectations. You can't get frustrated if your team isn't hitting daily goals if you didn't provide them guidance until two pm.

P.S. The day is over!

As you take a cup of the Prepared Brew, I want you to ask yourself:

- What do I need to take a better posture with to start my week?
- What are my NEED TO priorities?
- Where do I need to become more punctual?
- What is one thing I do really well from each category?

Subject: CPR Report

Free Space to write down key takeaways or answers to any questions found in this week's email:

_____

_____

_____

_____

Questions

Answer any challenging questions the email posed to you:

_____

_____

_____

_____

Challenge

What was the leadership challenge that spoke to you this week?

_____

_____

_____

_____

Perform

How do you plan to perform the challenges this week?

_____

_____

_____

_____

Repetitions

What do you need to do to remind yourself to get your reps in this week?

_____

_____

_____

_____

CPR Progress Report

(1 Needed Major Improvement - 5 CRUSHED IT!)

Rate yourself 1-5 on your leadership challenge this week

1   2   3   4   5

Rate 1-5 how well do you think you performed this week

1   2   3   4   5

Rate 1-5 how often you feel like you were consistent with your reps this week

1   2   3   4   5

Subject: Readiness Compound

This week, we are going to uncover our original Readiness Compound. I love the word *readiness*. It's the state of being fully prepared. Imagine if we could ready our teams every day. How many pressure points do you think you would be able to clear up for them? How about yourself?

With the three key ingredients, you can expect to heighten your team's state of readiness.

Readiness Compound (How you prepare your team)

- Reasonable- Setting goals and expectations can be challenging sometimes. Being reasonable isn't often a thought we have when setting goals or setting our teams up for success. We often want to shoot for the big goals; the ones that will get us noticed; the ones that you will get the promotion for. Let me ask you a question: Can you sustain those unreasonable big goals? John Wooden said, "It's the little details that are vital. Little things make big things happen." Think about that for a second. If you set goals of consistency, do you not think then month to month small positive changes will happen? I would rather be net positive five to ten members every month. Then plus thirty for one month. Because at the end of the year, I am going to be the big winner. Be reasonable when setting your goals. There are so many factors in setting reasonable goals. I am going to give you a few items to think about.

- Are you staffed to handle the goals?

- Is your team competent enough to achieve the goal?

- Do you know what's really important in your business?

- Is there another route you can try to achieve the desired outcome (instead of just focusing on retention)?

Set reasonable goals often. I am talking small chunks daily; this could even be per person. If the goal is $500 of revenue for the day and you have three people working, each person needs to shoot for $170 in their shift. Instead of saying the goal for the month is $15,000 of new revenue, break it down and make it reasonable. Being reasonable will make you more relatable.

- Reflect- Set an attitude of reflection in your studios. How often do you ask your team to reflect on the week? Here are a few reflection questions you can use with your team.
- What were some wins we had and why do we feel that way?
- What were some losses we had and how do we feel we can improve on them?
- What routines have we allowed to become a buzzkill on our teams?
- Did we set the right goals for the week?
- Did we meet, exceed, or fall below expectations last week?

Too often, we allow a behavior of complacency to set into our teams. This could be catastrophic without a reflection period to identify what's causing it. This is where we have to ask the reflection questions. Allow your team to answer and offer possible solutions. Everyone wants to be part of the solution. However, sometimes when you are too close to the problem, it's hard to identify there is one. I would suggest a weekly reflection session.

- Redirect- Everyone gets distracted from time to time and that's okay. We are all guilty of drifting. The problem is when drifting turns into roaming. This is where redirecting comes in to preparing your teams for readiness. A lot of what you will end up doing is redirecting behavior and habits. This is usually done after the reflection stage. We have to identify the problem, then redirect. There is one major player in redirecting. Always start with the why question. All change will have to start with *why*. Teams want to know what behavior is being redirected. It could be a simple behavior change like getting credit card info over the phone. Until our team understands why it's important, you will never redirect them. That's just a small example of why you must redirect with a why.

Take some time and set out three objectives you can do to help your team with their readiness.

Are you being reasonable?

How can you make your goals look and sound more reasonable?

Do you reflect at the end of the week?

Think about starting a ten-minute reflection phone call at the end of the week.

When was the last time you missed an opportunity to redirect a behavior?

Why did you miss it?

What *why* does your team need to hear?

bject: **CPR Report**

Free Space to write down key takeaways or answers to any questions found in this week's email:

_____

_____

_____

_____

Questions

Answer any challenging questions the email posed to you:

_____

_____

_____

_____

Challenge

What was the leadership challenge that spoke to you this week?

_____

_____

_____

_____

Perform

How do you plan to perform the challenges this week?

_____

_____

_____

_____

Repetitions

What do you need to do to remind yourself to get your reps in this week?

_____

_____

_____

_____

CPR Progress Report

(1 Needed Major Improvement - 5 CRUSHED IT!)

Rate yourself 1-5 on your leadership challenge this week

1   2   3   4   5

Rate 1-5 how well do you think you performed this week

1   2   3   4   5

Rate 1-5 how often you feel like you were consistent with your reps this week

1   2   3   4   5

Endurance Infusion

Our final week is super fitting. Because by this point, you are going to need a little extra endurance. Now that we have prepared ourselves and our teams, it's time to add a little staying power. Remember that power pre-game speech that got you so jacked up walking out of the locker room? Imagine putting that on repeat in your headset.

How do we extend the influence and motivation from the preparation? With the final three ingredients in the Endurance Infusion Blend.

Endurance Infusion Blend

- Engagement- I saw percentages of disengaged employees range from 47 percent to 87 percent in different surveys across the web. All those numbers are from different type of businesses and demographics. I don't believe they are wrong from what I have seen. How do we fix it? I don't think we will ever have 100 percent engagement 100 percent of the time. I do believe we can encourage engagement more often. I think it starts with communication. To engage with you, I have to be able to communicate with you. For instance, pull your team into the conversation. Ask for their ideas and solutions. When we started the Coach Advisory Board, it was all about bringing them into the conversation. The more we can communicate on all topics, the level of engagement will rise. I believe step two is to foster a culture of teamwork. I think in any team environment, you have engagement. Teammates know they are in it together, have each other's backs, and keep each other accountable. I think we try and overcomplicate employee engagement. Think about this stat from Corporate Leadership Council, "Employees who are committed and engaged at work perform 20 percent better and are 87 percent less likely to leave their current company."

Keep it simple with communication and a culture of teamwork and collaboration.

- Encourage- Being a fitness coach for a long time, I know the hidden power of encouragement. For eighteen years, my daily vocabulary was all based around words of encouragement. *Encourage* is a verb; it's an action. It's the action of giving support. This doesn't have come by way of motivational quotes. It literally means *give support.* Now words of encouragement never hurt, but think about making eye contact with someone. Just acknowledging them is encouraging. Listen, I mean really listen. Fist bumps when they do little things. Air horns when they do big things. Encouragement will also help with your engagement levels.

- Evaluate- Lastly, people want to know where they stand. Ensure you are providing frequent evaluations. These don't have to be in-depth or lengthy. These are simple pulse checks with your team. What are some soft skills you are teaching your team? Evaluate those soft skills. We have the new employee onboarding training. Once they pass Angela's first week of training, you get this brand-new employee and, for their first five shifts, you are training but more so *evaluating*. Don't think of an evaluation as something you are checking on in the past. Evaluate the mood of the studio. Evaluations should be done frequently with and without notice. Evaluations help encourage your teams. This is the act of supporting them.

Now that you have read the entire label of that supplement bottle, you are ready to take that first scoop of blue raspberry juice.

Give some endurance behind your motivation by asking yourself these questions:

How engaged is your staff?

Where do you need to improve engagement, communication, or teamwork?

Pick three team members this week to encourage.

- Sit and listen to one
- Acknowledge the achievement of another
- Give another a little pep talk

It's probably time you did a few evaluations. Pick two team members to evaluate this week.

Subject: CPR Report

Free Space to write down key takeaways or answers to any questions found in this week's email:

_____

_____

_____

_____

Questions

Answer any challenging questions the email posed to you:

_____

_____

_____

_____

Challenge

What was the leadership challenge that spoke to you this week?

_____

_____

_____

_____

Perform

How do you plan to perform the challenges this week?

_____

_____

_____

_____

Repetitions

What do you need to do to remind yourself to get your reps in this week?

_____

_____

_____

_____

CPR Progress Report

(1 Needed Major Improvement - 5 CRUSHED IT!)

Rate yourself 1-5 on your leadership challenge this week

1   2   3   4   5

Rate 1-5 how well do you think you performed this week

1   2   3   4   5

Rate 1-5 how often you feel like you were consistent with your reps this week

1   2   3   4   5

Subject: **Corn Maze**

Fall is my favorite time of year. I grew up in the north, going to fall festivals, haunted houses, and corn mazes. Since moving to Florida, fall is usually lumped in with our elongated summer, which I am not complaining about.

However, fall just doesn't feel like fall to me. Fortunately, with this little break in the weather we have had, I have been in full fall mode.

Faith and I decided to go explore one of the local farms that has a nine-acre corn maze. A blast of the past. We enjoyed the wafting scent of kettle corn, hitting us on a breeze that was just cool enough to keep the sweat off, but not quite cool enough for long sleeves.

As we walked through this massive corn maze, along with the laughs, the flashlight batteries went on and off, and the feeling of nostalgia. Oh, and a few wrong turns which led us right back to the same post marker we had just come from.

It got me thinking about how easy it is to get lost in the maze of leadership.

We didn't go into this maze completely blind. We had some resources. A picture of the maze from above (a map of sorts), we had a flashlight (not a great one, but it was a light), lastly each other (a team).

As leaders, we also have access to resources. The question is: do we sometimes forget we have them or forget the value they can provide us?

We had these tools in our possession from the time we entered into the maze. However, we only found ourselves using them when we got into some trouble.

I have seen leaders with large stocks of resources available to them, only to see so many forget they have them. Or forget the benefits that will come from the assistance of those resources.

What I would like to do is break down the corn maze leadership tool kit, what you need and the benefit of each tool. As you navigate your own maze, I believe these three tools will have you gracefully walking across the finish line of the maze in a lot less time, and with more laughs and less irritation.

Map

A map is critical in this situation, especially when it's dark and the corn stalks are above your head. A map provides you with a forecast, which leads to efficiency and proper execution.

On your leadership map, there is a vital detail you must have, if you want your team to escape the maze.

You need checkpoints. Just because you are following the map doesn't mean you made all the right turns, or the turns in order. It's important your team hits checkpoints. Checkpoints provide confidence to continue on the path they are on. Without checkpoints, you will have uncertainty, even with the security of the map.

Flashlight

When it's dark and not much moonlight, it's easy to run into a dead-end. Even a flashlight with dying batteries will work.

See, a flashlight only works when you want it to. As leaders, sometimes we don't want to turn on the light, because we may see problems we either aren't prepared for or don't want to deal with. However, by doing this, you leave your team in the dark and lead them into a dead-end. What you are also doing is slowing progress.

With a light and a map, you and your team can move much quicker, because you can see obstacles that may be coming up. You also protect your team from the discouragement of dead-ends. No one likes to hit dead-ends, so shine a light on the dead-ends in your maze.

Communication

Lastly, we all know how important it is to communicate. I want to touch quickly on timely communication. Faith did a great job with telling me, "Okay, at the end, we are going to take a right, then an immediate left, from there we will walk straight for a bit." By communicating a few steps ahead, it gave me more confidence to move a little quicker. I wasn't looking at the map. So without her communication, I would have been lost. Or if Faith communicated a turn too late, I could have made a wrong turn and had to correct course.

This form of communication only works if you trust the person giving you directions. Does your team trust you enough to blindly walk by your directions only, with no map or flashlight?

If you can look at your business as a corn maze this month, create a map for your team. What are the checkpoints that allow them to know they are on the right track and hitting them in order?

Provide some light so your team can travel a little quicker without running into or over obstacles. However, there may be some obstacles you need to clear out of the way first.

Lastly, create an undeniable trust with your team. Allow timely communication without hesitation.

Subject: CPR Report

Free Space to write down key takeaways or answers to any questions found in this week's email:

_____

_____

_____

_____

Questions

Answer any challenging questions the email posed to you:

_____

_____

_____

_____

Challenge

What was the leadership challenge that spoke to you this week?

_____

_____

_____

_____

Perform

How do you plan to perform the challenges this week?

_____

_____

_____

_____

Repetitions

What do you need to do to remind yourself to get your reps in this week?

_____

_____

_____

_____

CPR Progress Report

(1 Needed Major Improvement - 5 CRUSHED IT!)

Rate yourself 1-5 on your leadership challenge this week

1   2   3   4   5

Rate 1-5 how well do you think you performed this week

1   2   3   4   5

Rate 1-5 how often you feel like you were consistent with your reps this week

1   2   3   4   5

Subject: Do You Know About F.A.L.L.?

You guys know already how big of a fall junkie I am. Give me all the fall things. As I was in studios this past week, I saw a common theme.

You guys also know I write things down; no one else can even attempt to read my handwriting but it's all there.

As I was reviewing my week and what I heard, saw, and wrote, it was so clear to me, almost as clear as nice, cool fall morning with no humidity, no clouds in the sky, virtually no wind.

It was right there in front of me—F.A.L.L. I kid you not. I was going to write something this week about pumpkin carving. So, that's on hold now.

Where do leaders F.A.L.L.? We get so caught up in the whirlwind of our days, especially in our environments.

We end up tripping and catching ourselves and tripping and catching ourselves, until finally you trip and lose yourself and FALL.

Sometimes no one sees it. Other times just a few of your team see it. Other times you FALL in front of an audience.

Okay we get it, so you have an acronym for F.A.L.L. How cute. No, how necessary. How necessary to be able to see the crack in the sidewalk before we FALL. No one likes to fall in private. Think about falling in front of a stadium packed with people.

Okay, hopefully you don't want to FALL now, or ever. But how do you prevent it?

Utilize these four easy-to-remember strategies:

Follow Up
Accountability
Love
Lead by Example

Let's unpack the first two this week.

Usually when you are about to FALL, it starts with an object causing you to trip. This object as a leader is Follow Up. It's like that piece of sidewalk that a tree root has grown under and caused the cement to rise higher than the other pieces. Before you know it, that sidewalk grabs the toe of your shoe and you are on your way to the ground.

So how do we avoid the obstacle of Follow Up? Below you will find five simple steps to follow to avoid the first step of the FALL.

Follow up on:

Performance Expectations

- Does your team understand the why behind their goals?

  - Just giving arbitrary goals doesn't motivate anyone.

- Inspect what you expect

  - Audit expectations you expect are being done consistently.

- Find areas of fog

- Ask where you need to clear things up.

- Training Opportunities

  - Where does your team need continued training?

- Feedback Loop

  - Provide feedback often based on not meeting the expectations.

Accountability in the FALL is where you brain kicks in and begins to alert your body to brace for impact. Sometimes we walk around without that heightened sense of awareness. It only kicks in when it's too late, when we are already failing.

Is it possible to have a heightened sense of awareness all the time? The good news is the answer is yes... but the bad news is, it's not easy. Accountability is one of the toughest areas of leadership for most leaders.

When most people think of accountability, they immediately go to the negative. They think it has to be a tough conversation, or confrontation. This couldn't be farther from the truth.

Accountability is a team having a shared purpose. This is why I love the Four Disciplines of Execution and how they talk about accountability.

Cadence of Accountability (from the Four Disciplines of Execution)

Create a Weekly Accountability Session

- Weekly meeting lasting no longer than twenty minutes with a set agenda

- Focus of session

  - to hold each other accountable for weekly commitments of actions that will move the lead measures

- This meeting should be the same time every week.
- The whirlwind is never allowed into this session, no matter how urgent it may be.

Weekly Commitments

- Big Question: "What can we do this week to impact the lead measures?"

  - Each weekly commitment must meet three standards:

    - Represent a specific deliverable

      - Commitment to exactly what you will do, when you will do it, and how you expect the outcome will be.

    - Must influence a lead measure

    - Timely

Agenda for Sessions
- Account

  - Report on Commitments

- Review the Scoreboard

  - Learn from success and failures

- Plan

  - Clear the path and make new commitments

Why does this work so well?

Because your team is making commitments to each other. They are being held accountable not just by their direct report but also by their peers. They must be able to stand in front of their teams and either say they helped their teams or they didn't make good on their commitments.

No one wants to be the player that holds their team back.

Let's create team players by creating a cadence of accountability. This will not only heighten your senses but will also allow you to avoid uneven sidewalks.

Next week, team, we will look at love and leading by example.

bject: CPR Report

Free Space to write down key takeaways or answers to any
questions found in this week's email:

_____

_____

_____

_____

Questions

Answer any challenging questions the email posed to you:

_____

_____

_____

_____

Challenge

What was the leadership challenge that spoke to you
this week?

_____

_____

_____

_____

Perform

How do you plan to perform the challenges this week?

_____

_____

_____

_____

Repetitions

What do you need to do to remind yourself to get your reps in this week?

_____

_____

_____

_____

CPR Progress Report

(1 Needed Major Improvement - 5 CRUSHED IT!)

Rate yourself 1-5 on your leadership challenge this week

1   2   3   4   5

Rate 1-5 how well do you think you performed this week

1   2   3   4   5

Rate 1-5 how often you feel like you were consistent with your reps this week

1   2   3   4   5

We have been falling for about a week right now. It's about
time we stopped FALLing. Last week, we talked about the
F being that piece of sidewalk that grabs the toe of your
shoe and starts the process of falling. Or, as I called it the
Follow Up process—one that we should revisit as often
as daily just to check in. There is no harm in following up.
Trust me, if it wasn't for the follow up, I wouldn't be going
on ten years of marriage. Another story for another time.

Secondly, we addressed the A. Accountability translated
is your awareness that you are falling. The heightened
sense of panic you feel when your brain lets the rest of
your body know to brace for impact. Setting up the loop
of accountability is such a crucially important element of
maintaining expectations.

So I know what you're thinking. I have already tripped and I
know I am falling. What else is there to know about falling?

I'm glad you are thinking that. There are two more steps:
Love and Lead, which are the last two topics in this
email series.

Before I get to that, do me a favor as you are reading this—
stop. Open a notebook or grab a piece of paper. Now get
a pen... write down what last week's email helped you with
the most this week. How did you implement either the F or
the A, leading your team this week? Once you have done
that, give yourself a score of 1-5. One is what we talked
about it Monday and I just got caught in the whirlwind and
forgot it by Tuesday. Five being I was able to circle back
each day and be consistent.

Next, write down if you noticed anything different once you added either the F or the A. Lastly, how do you plan to stay consistent this week with it?

Okay, now that we have exercised your brains a little, let's dive into the Ls.

The first L is the bracing for the fall. The body is notified and begins to tense up. The more prepared for the impact, the better a possible outcome. See if we stay relaxed that could cause some serious damage when we hit the ground.

However, to be effective and get out of harm's way of the impact, we need to embrace that this is where love comes in.

I want to highlight two areas of love and leadership. I know you are probably thinking I'm going to get sappy on you. I don't know, maybe keep reading to find out.

Do you love your WHY and does your team love their WHY?

It sounds very much like every other leadership book/blog/podcast. Love what you do and this and that. Well, I want to take a little different approach. Let's talk about your WHY first and why that's important.

If the leader doesn't LOVE WHY, they are in their role or position. Then you will never care enough to make changes to your leadership style and help others.

Love is such a strong word.

- To me, love means never taking the shortcut. Shortcuts usually take us around obstacles. The problem is you'll never address them if you are always avoiding them.

- Love is being able to sit down and self-reflect, and recognize areas you can improve. You do this because of others.

- Love has no concept of time.

- Love can't count money. Think about this; if you can't love your spouse when you have little money, do you think a lot of money will make it easier? Let me try it for those who aren't married. If you don't love your job making a little money, more money won't make you love it either.

It's extremely hard to lead without a love for why you do what you do.

It's next to impossible to lead a staff who doesn't love their why.

So I'll ask you this: Whose WHY meter is running low inside your studio? Is it yours or theirs? How can you refuel it?

That brings us to our last L. The final part of the FALL. This is the most hurtful part. This is more of the physiological effect of the fall. This is the embarrassment of laying on the ground while others managed to get over the cracked sidewalk. It's when you start to wonder why you didn't see it earlier. How you could have prevented the tear in your jeans, scuffed palms, and the puddle of embarrassment you are lying in?

I believe as leaders when we get out of practice of leading by example, we lose touch with the instincts. Ever felt like your team has a better handle on a situation than you do? Ever feel like when you are making a sale you find it hard to follow the same processes you expect your staff to? Leading by example keeps you sharp and well-oiled.

So how can you stay sharp and well-oiled? I'm glad you asked. Think about your favorite knife or your car. Your knives should be sharpened every three to four months, your car usually needs an oil change about the same. While you use them daily, they still need maintenance.

This is how I want to address leading by example.

First, you should take the time and be in the trenches doing the job shoulder to shoulder with your team. This is keeping your skills sharp and also they are watching you and learning from that shared experience.

Stephen Covey said, "What you do has far greater impact than what you say."

Every three to four months, you need a sharpen-your-skills session. Talk to a mentor, read a new book, listen to a podcast, find a conference. If your team sees you're in pursuit to become a better leader, they will find value in this skill development as well.

Leading by example isn't always about doing the job next to someone. It's developing new sets of skills so you increase the capacity of your team.

I want you to do me a favor. Pull your phone out. Pull up the alarm, set it for three minutes from now. Turn your phone off and just be still and quiet. Reflect on the last two weeks. When the time goes off, I want you to write down whatever came to you. Try and write for another three minutes.

Create an environment where you are the CSO, the Chief Sidewalk Officer, and you are leading your team down a smooth sidewalk. Your job is to pave the way for your team so they can avoid tripping up. When those cracks do show up, you now have a game plan on getting you and your team over them safely and without bloody knees.

Subject: CPR Report

Free Space to write down key takeaways or answers to any questions found in this week's email:

_____

_____

_____

_____

Questions

Answer any challenging questions the email posed to you:

_____

_____

_____

_____

Challenge

What was the leadership challenge that spoke to you this week?

_____

_____

_____

_____

Perform

How do you plan to perform the challenges this week?

_____

_____

_____

_____

Repetitions

What do you need to do to remind yourself to get your reps in this week?

_____

_____

_____

_____

CPR Progress Report

(1 Needed Major Improvement - 5 CRUSHED IT!)

Rate yourself 1-5 on your leadership challenge this week

1   2   3   4   5

Rate 1-5 how well do you think you performed this week

1   2   3   4   5

Rate 1-5 how often you feel like you were consistent with your reps this week

1   2   3   4   5

Subject: **Managing Candy**

Trick or treat, give me something good to eat. Oh man, I can remember dressing up like a Michigan University football player. I would have a black eye and a bloody nose. Looking back, not sure if I was a dead player or I just got beat up a lot on the field. Either way, I was always so stoked to grab that pillowcase and set out with the cast of spooky characters on the block.

It always seemed to be a contest of who could collect the most candy; not just the most candy but the holy grail was full-sized candy bars. If you walked away with a full-sized Butterfinger, you won.

When the fire whistle would sound, trick-or-treating came to an end. Then candy management took place. This is where all of us would dump out our pillowcases of a night's hard work, then start to take an inventory of all the different kinds of candy we scored that night. There were piles of bright-colored candy wrappers all over the floor.

Candy management—this got me thinking about managing people if they were candy. Imagine you went trick-or-treating for employees and you took an inventory of your teams. Do you have any of these candies below?

If so, I have good news for you. I also included how to manage each type of candy. After years of candy management, I thought I would share some ideas.

Sour Patch Kids—these are your team members who have the sour then sweet attitudes. These can be frustrating team members to manage, because you never know if sour or sweet is walking in. When they are sweet, you enjoy every second they are in your studio. They are major influencers on the team and in the business. They tend to set the tone when they are on shift. When the sweet SPK shows up, work gets done and positivity is high.

When they are sour, not only are they not productive, but they infect the rest of the team members. When sour, they can be real energy vampires. Jon Gordon says, "No energy vampires allowed."

So how do you deal with the SPKs/

- Turn *problems* into *possibilities*

  - Sour SPKs will look for problems specifically.

  - They are so focused on problems, they don't see possibilities.

  - They don't even realize their own possibilities.

- Change the "*Have to*" attitude to a "*Get to*" attitude

  - Sour SPKs attitude is likely a "Have to."

  - Truth is you don't have to do anything, we get to.

- Avoid *Gripes* and focus on *Goals*

  - SPKs tend to gripe and, over time, that will eat away at you.

  - If you give them goals, they can use their influence to help everyone achieve goals.

- *Validate* over *dictate*

  - SPKs always accept validation, so recognize them and make them feel valued.

- SPKs don't like to be spoken down to.

- This doesn't mean let them walk all over you. Find the balance of validation and support.

Smarties — these are the know-it-all employees. I don't say that in a bad way. Hear me out. Smarties are the highly competent employees, the ones who don't usually ask for what to do next. They are good problem-solvers and can identify problems before they pop up.

So, you are probably wondering, what's the catch? With Smarties, there is one major issue you need to know and look out for.

Smarties are sensitive to feedback. They tend to be self-confident individuals, and we don't want to tear that down when we give feedback to them. Remember the three tips below when giving a Smartie feedback.

- Face the problem head on

  - They are smart enough to know when you are trying to have a constructive conversation.

  - Don't beat around the bush with a Smartie.

- Ask them questions

  - Don't just present the facts. Chances are they already know them.

  - If they don't, it's a great way to find out what they know and don't know by asking questions.

  - Always make sure they know the correct answer and, more importantly, the why.

- Focus on solutions with Smarties

- You need to address the issue but do it by way of providing or asking for a solution for the problem.

- Smarties usually like to fix issues.

- Let them help.

Laffy Taffy—these are the team members who are always down for a good time. They are the ones who will make you laugh and, at the same time, totally distract the rest of the team. LTs enjoy coming to work but don't always enjoy work. The other great trait of LTs is they tend to stick around. Okay, so you are probably thinking these team members are going to be a handful. The answer is yes. However, I am going to say LTs could be your biggest asset if you learn how to use their enthusiasm to your advantage.

LTs like to have fun; they are most likely competitive as well. If you can tie in some fun game-based play into their goals and daily production, you will win the game at engaging LTs during their shift.

LTs also have to know they have the freedom to joke and have fun, but you have to lay down the boundaries. If not, they will push and push to see how much they can get away with.

How to Win with LTs

- Make work and goals fun and competitive.

- Have a scoreboard everyone can see and interact with.

- Updated your scoreboard consistently to keep them tuned in.

- Maybe you have a staff daily riddle and you allow your LT to come up with it.

- Set boundaries for fun

  - Example: LTs clock in and the first 10-15 minutes of their shift let them get whatever it is out of their system.

  - Example: When you achieve X goal on your shift, you get three shots at the Nerf basketball hoop.

  - Then refocus their enthusiasm on the daily scoreboard and the game at hand.

Good and Plenty—this is the team member who is satisfied with the bare minimum. They have the *good and plenty* attitude. Do you have someone who completes all their standard tasks and then puts on the cruise control for the rest of their shift? They have this is the *plenty enough for today* mindset.

This person isn't always a bad employee. To be honest, most of us right now would love someone who completes all their tasks. So, it's learning how to work with these good and plenty's. It's not a personality problem; it's a priority problem. Their priorities are completing all the tasks. This is the G&P mindset. If we can focus them on completing the important tasks to help move the team forward, the G&P's can add a huge amount of value to our team. Think of the word urgency here. While completing all daily tasks are important, if we were able to put some urgency behind an objective, that is going to drive a specific KPI. Then make that the focus and your G&P will complete that task. So, you may have to try something a little different when setting goals for G&Ps. Think about the word *plenty*, "more than enough." This can be confusing because we would think a large quantity is a good thing. More is better right? Wrong. With a G&P, more than enough is subjective to the G&P, not you. When they feel they have done, "more than enough," they throw in the towel for the day.

How to motivate G&P's

- Set priorities on daily tasks that will drive metrics.

    - Leads

    - Sales

    - Booking Appointments

- Create Urgency

    - How many?

    - When does it need to be completed by?

Take a quick inventory of your candy. Find out how you may need to change how you manage it!

Three steps this week:

1. Write down which type of team members you have.

2. Next to their name and candy type, write down a strategy to help lead them more effectively.

3. Write down the next steps for better candy management on a consistent basis.

Subject: **CPR Report**

Free Space to write down key takeaways or answers to any questions found in this week's email:

_____
_____
_____
_____

Questions

Answer any challenging questions the email posed to you:

_____
_____
_____
_____

Challenge

What was the leadership challenge that spoke to you this week?

_____
_____
_____
_____

Perform

How do you plan to perform the challenges this week?

_____

_____

_____

_____

Repetitions

What do you need to do to remind yourself to get your reps in this week?

_____

_____

_____

_____

CPR Progress Report

(1 Needed Major Improvement - 5 CRUSHED IT!)

Rate yourself 1-5 on your leadership challenge this week

1   2   3   4   5

Rate 1-5 how well do you think you performed this week

1   2   3   4   5

Rate 1-5 how often you feel like you were consistent with your reps this week

1   2   3   4   5

Subject: Chlorophyll Levels

As you all know, Faith and I were in the mountains of North Georgia this past week to celebrate our ten-year anniversary.

You also know I love the fall time and, ironically, we got married on October 30th.

You are probably wondering why that's important.

Well, it's the perfect time to see the leaves change colors. Being from Florida now, for the past five years our palm trees don't change color with the seasons. By the way, not complaining, just facts.

As I was sitting on the back porch of our cabin, I started to think about how leadership can take on different shades of color.

Before we dive into that, let's take a quick trip back to middle school science class. Why do leaves change color?

The days in the fall get shorter and there is less sunlight, and the temperatures change. Therefore, the leaves stop the process of making food for itself. The chlorophyll breaks down and the green color fades. Then the brilliant shades of orange, yellow, and reds begin to show up.

It's so interesting that those are the colors that leaves turn into when they are going dormant and die off.

As I said earlier, I believe there are different shades to leadership and these shades can become a foreshadowing of what's to come if you start to lack the proper leadership nutrients.

What I want to do is break down these colors and give you some insight of the stage you may be in and how to use or overcome each stage. We don't want anyone falling off the tree!

Stage One Green:

This is where you are vibrant and full of life. You are able to maintain your level of energy and enthusiasm, while keeping up with the daily tasks inside and outside of work. Don't think of this as work/life balance, but more as proper energy management. Staying green also comes with staff's energy and enthusiasm. The more energetic your team is, the longer you can stay green.

How do you get into or stay in the green:

First would come with energy management. You have to be able to prioritize your day. Above all this will help you manage your energy as a leader.

Second, serve your team. Become the servant leader your team needs. Nothing will get your team excited and enthusiastic than a leader who has their backs.

Think about the little things. When is the last time you bought your team coffee? When is the last time you wrote them a thank-you note? When is the last time you said a shout-out for them for something little they did (like cleaning the windows, not always sales)?

The little things will keep you green as well as your team.

Stage Two Orange:

This is where the leader is trying to do all the things. They think BIG things will make the difference. Big things take a lot of energy, which you can do for a little amount of time. You are trying to be your business, members, and teams' number-one hype person. The only problem is you can't sustain that. Believe it or not, everyone knows it too and they are just waiting for the battery meter to run out.

You can use stage two for the jumpstart, kind of like jumper cables. The battery just needs a little juice to turn over. There are times you need a little bit of orange leadership.

How to use stage two properly:

Use it when you need it. When you see signs that some element of your business needs the jumper cables, throw them on and turn over that part of the business, but then quickly take off the cables. This will ensure it's not just you giving the power. But that part of the business isn't dead; it just needs a little jump.

Orange is a vibrant energetic color; however in the color scale, it sits between yellow and red, which you will see the danger of swinging too far one direction can bring.

Stage Three Yellow:

This is preservation mode. This is where you are just trying to survive. You have lost the enthusiasm and motivation. You have become an anxious leader.

Stage three is like a yellow light. You either jam on the gas or pound on the brakes. In one case, you rev your engine and chance running a red light, so you increase the amount of anxiety you have, which doesn't help in preservation mode. Chances are you are already anxious, because you are not able to keep up with all your responsibilities or you feel your team is falling apart. As a leader, these worries can lead to thoughts of job security and really start to question your position, and if you are performing well or not. You see, that's the thing about anxiety; it keeps you in preservation mode. You are paralyzed to not really move out of the pit you have dug for yourself. Trust me, I know a little about bouts of anxiety. Anxiety and excitement have very similar physiological responses. However, they cause your brain to respond very differently. An anxious brain doesn't want to move, it wants to preserve; where an excited brain can't wait to move forward.

Preservation mode is very dangerous for any leader. Your team starts to suffer because then they begin trying to figure out how to fend for themselves. The business suffers because the little things are nonexistent. This is due to only having enough in the tank for the big-ticket items.

Is there a leadership Xanax?

There actually is, and it doesn't come with unwanted side effects. It's fairly simple as well.

First, you need to reach out for help. This is the hardest part. Stage three likes to hide in the shadows and those dark places can keep you from asking for help. ASK! Just talking to someone can be a big first step.

Second, create some consistency in your routine. Consistency will help you hit the green lights and avoid yellows. This seems so simple, but it's not. Do me a favor and try to set three things that you want to do every day this week. This is the first step to prioritizing and getting your leadership back on track.

Stage Four Red:

Now, on the flip side, you pound down on the break. This is what leads you into stage four. This leads to frustrated leaders. This is the total burn out stage. The problem with stage four is you don't know it till it's too late. This is the yellow light that turned red quickly and now you're stuck. When I hit this stage years ago, my good friend told me, "A fire truck on fire is no good to anyone." That's essentially the stage four in a sentence. Remember I was telling you the danger of living in the orange and swinging one way or the other. Living in the orange too long will push you into the red. I need to provide some warning signs for you. The scary problem with this stage is sometimes you don't even know you are there.

Warning signs:

- Don't look forward to going to work.
- Can't stand being there when you do go.
- Everyone and everything gets on your nerves.
- You become angry and spiteful with people.
- Joy is totally gone.
- You lost total connection with your team.

How can you prevent this dangerous zone? In addition to the above recommendations at each stage:

Self-care is most important here. I am talking about two different types of self-care.

First, take some time off! Take a day or a weekend off. Disconnect and recharge your batteries.

Self-care on a regular basis. Do at least one thing each day you enjoy. Fill your personal tank, whatever it is. Mine is working out and reading or writing.

Second, self-care is making sure you are still passionate about what you are doing, and why you are doing it.

If you have lost the passion for what you do, why you are doing it? Who you are doing it for? Then it's time to make a choice. Staying in the red zone isn't helping anyone, especially you.

Take some time and do a self-audit of where you might be currently. What do you need to do to overcome the stage you are in and stay attached to the tree?

Team, let's stay vibrant and full of life this week.

Our team just went through a very high energy week and possibly needs a little refueling. Do something for them this week.

Subject: **CPR Report**

Free Space to write down key takeaways or answers to any questions found in this week's email:

_____

_____

_____

_____

Questions

Answer any challenging questions the email posed to you:

_____

_____

_____

_____

Challenge

What was the leadership challenge that spoke to you this week?

_____

_____

_____

_____

Perform

How do you plan to perform the challenges this week?

_____

_____

_____

_____

Repetitions

What do you need to do to remind yourself to get your reps in this week?

_____

_____

_____

_____

CPR Progress Report

(1 Needed Major Improvement - 5 CRUSHED IT!)

Rate yourself 1-5 on your leadership challenge this week

1   2   3   4   5

Rate 1-5 how well do you think you performed this week

1   2   3   4   5

Rate 1-5 how often you feel like you were consistent with your reps this week

1   2   3   4   5

Subject: Up, Up Away

Can you imagine wrestling with a 400-pound astronaut Snoopy? This balloon is four stories tall, and as wide as six taxi cabs. He is just one of eighteen larger-than-life balloons in this year's Macy's Thanksgiving Day parade.

Did you know there is actually a balloon flying school and a whole selection process? Well, first you have to be a Macy's employee or have a sponsor. Then there are physical requirements: they look at the height and weight of the handlers as well as their physical fitness and stamina. They not only need a strong core, arms, and back. They also need to be able to walk at least 2.5 miles, while keeping Snoopy from being swept up by the wind that whips through the city's skyscrapers.

Then after you are selected, you go to balloon boot camp. This is a pretty serious process.

I have been in NYC and watched the parade in person. I can tell you it looked hard. But what was most impressive was the handlers' teamwork.

Each balloon has anywhere from 50, but most have 100 team members. That's a lot of people who are all involved in the safety and security of their balloons.

They don't only walk forward without stopping. No, they are sometimes doing circles and making their balloon snoopy arms wave. They also have to hold their positions sometime and wait for the parade to start back up again. This is not an individual sprint by any means. This is a true test of teamwork and communication.

Teamwork was a big topic of conversation at this past week's leadership meeting.

Which is why I started to think about these massive balloons and the teams who handle them. I believe there are three attributes that a team must have to successfully fly their balloons.

First is they must have a shared vision. Think about the balloon for a moment.

Every handler can see the road ahead and any possible obstacles that may be in the way. They all have the vision of walking this balloon down the path of the parade, without hitting any buildings or the balloon breaking loose.

It is essential that we share our vision with the entire team. They need to be able to see the destination ahead; this is as important short term as long term.

Think about sharing a daily vision with your teams. This way, their job performance becomes a shared vision instead of just meeting daily expectations. If everyone catches the vision for the day/week/month, you will have more people understanding how their role is vital in the shared vision. You can't have some handlers walking forward, others stopping, and then others trying to do circles. While one of the expectations is being met, don't let go of the rope. The synergy of the vision is off. You need a shared vision to bring synergy into your team performance.

Secondly, you need shared commitment. The very definition of commitment should be all the explanation we need for this segment: "The state or quality of being dedicated to a cause, activity, etc."

With a shared vision, I then need shared commitments to the cause or activity. This can be done by getting a verbal commitment from your team members to each other.

The balloon handlers know the commitment of their teammates. They understand each other's role and how it impacts the team. This is ultimately how we can easily keep our teams accountable. When your team commits to being a part of the vision, then their role is on display. It's hard to be held accountable when you don't step up and step out.

When was the last time you had your team make commitments to each other, and display those commitments publicly? This is not a shaming effort; this is an effort to help boost the commitment of each member of the team.

Lastly, there is shared experience. When the team has the vision and commits to the actions or cause, they can then enjoy the experience along the way.

Have you ever seen how happy those balloon handlers are? They love what they are doing. It's because the first two steps are aligned.

Why is a shared experience so important?

Each team member feels their work and commitment contributes to the shared vision. As well, each member feels everyone is committed and pulling their fair share along the way!

This is where we can have a truly shared experience. More than likely, the shared experience is a positive outcome and they can all feel it; not like most teams where one person always feels like they are putting more effort in here or there; not really knowing what happens when they aren't on shift because they don't know what commitments others have made.

Shared experience makes for a smooth and enjoyable balloon ride.

A shared experience will lead to a feeling of accomplishment and excitement.

This week, I would challenge you to make sure your team has a vision for today, tomorrow, and Friday.

You have them make a commitment to their team.

Watch the team come together as they work toward a common goal with individual investment.

Subject: **CPR Report**

Free Space to write down key takeaways or answers to any questions found in this week's email:

_____

_____

_____

_____

Questions

Answer any challenging questions the email posed to you:

_____

_____

_____

Challenge

What was the leadership challenge that spoke to you this week?

_____

_____

_____

_____

Perform

How do you plan to perform the challenges this week?

_____

_____

_____

_____

Repetitions

What do you need to do to remind yourself to get your reps in this week?

_____

_____

_____

_____

CPR Progress Report

(1 Needed Major Improvement - 5 CRUSHED IT!)

Rate yourself 1-5 on your leadership challenge this week

1   2   3   4   5

Rate 1-5 how well do you think you performed this week

1   2   3   4   5

Rate 1-5 how often you feel like you were consistent with your reps this week

1   2   3   4   5

Subject: Big Dinner Game Plan

As Thanksgiving approaches, we have all started to plan out that big dinner. Maybe some of you have started collecting your supplies already, or at least started to make a list of what you are going to need.

If you are anything like my household, the table is already set and I know Faith already has a vision for how the food is going to be displayed before we eat it. There's a lineup for dishes we are going to need, including what needs to be cooked first, so the oven is ready when the next dish needs to go in.

For a knockdown Thanksgiving in my wife's family, you need a game plan. This isn't an hour here and an hour there. We are talking full-blown cooking for two to three days before the Macy's Day Parade even comes on.

You are probably thinking I'm going to talk about vision. Wrong! That would be the easy and not a well thought-out way to go.

Nope, much different actually, and it comes on the heels of our ASM conference call Friday. We were discussing topics like creating clear goals, and creating a proper accountability loop, and helping give the team a forecast of priorities.

As we were wrapping up what I feel was a super productive call, someone asked me about how I keep such an upbeat attitude all the time.

I led with *it's a choice*; which, yes, it absolutely is first and foremost. However, I started to think more about that question. As most of you know, my brain like a lot like yours;

it never stops, always self-reflecting on conversations and interactions I have.

When I was taking notes on what to write about this week, I started to dive a little deeper into the question that was asked and my quick response.

While I still do believe wholeheartedly is that positivity and attitude are a choice you make. I also believe having a game plan sets me up for success when it comes to choosing to have a positive attitude.

I was thinking about myself in the past. Some of the most negative times I had, I was the most lost. I could be driving to Disney and in such a good mood. Make a wrong turn and get lost and the whole attitude changes! I got thrown off my game.

Have you ever been thrown off your game and just feel irritable and frustrated, and you don't even know why?

I remember playing sports and going into each game, we had a game plan. The first ten plays were mapped out before we walked onto the field. Our attitudes were optimistic and positive. We knew exactly what we were getting into. The game plan allowed our minds to relax so we could choose to be positive.

Like when Faith prepares Thanksgiving dinner; there is no stress when she goes shopping. She has a game plan walking into the store. There are no mistakes in the kitchen because she has a game plan. The table and food presentation is what she pictured because she has a game plan.

This allows her to have a great attitude in the pressure of creating an amazing meal for all to enjoy.

What is it about a game plan that allows you to have a positive attitude?

Confidence!

After thinking about it, that's what really produces the upbeat and positive attitude. It's confidence.

When you wake up and know what your next three moves are before you get out of bed, it allows you to go about your day in the right mindset. Having a game plan enables your naturally negative self to stay asleep and you awaken your upbeat, positive attitude.

Walking into a day without a game plan is like taking a road trip with only a final destination and no directions in between. The stress of how to get there will ultimately cause the trip to become a negative experience quickly.

Let me ask: Do you set yourself up for success each day starting off with a big dose of confidence?

Let me give you three tips that I have found work well for me:

First, you need a planner or something to write in; one page for each day. Mine is split into three categories.

One... Top three, need to task before noon. I give myself a what and a when.

Two... other action items today usually limit it to five. Now these five could get shifted to tomorrow if need be.

Three... I brain dump ideas I had during the day and things I learned or areas we can continue to improve. I may also write who I need to email first thing the next day.

I know for me, I need to see items getting checked off the list. This keeps fueling my positive and upbeat attitude. There is nothing worse than being busy but not productive. I believe that will zap your attitude to the core. You feel tired and almost defeated, which is a big drain on your confidence.

Remember, you don't have to do all the things.

By creating a game plan, not only will it allow you to possibly do more of the things. It will allow for a better attitude while doing it.

Let's not forget your team. Imagine walking in and not having a game plan. How can we get mad at them if they are just showing up and blindly and mindlessly going about their day?

The game plan and attitude are trickle-down effects. When you can get yours in check, you will better serve your team with a game plan they can feel confident and excited about.

So, you want to show up to work with a smile and excitement? Do the prep work and have a game plan!

Subject: CPR Report

Free Space to write down key takeaways or answers to any questions found in this week's email:

_____

_____

_____

_____

Questions

Answer any challenging questions the email posed to you:

_____

_____

_____

_____

Challenge

What was the leadership challenge that spoke to you this week?

_____

_____

_____

_____

Perform

How do you plan to perform the challenges this week?

_____

_____

_____

_____

Repetitions

What do you need to do to remind yourself to get your reps in this week?

_____

_____

_____

_____

CPR Progress Report

(1 Needed Major Improvement - 5 CRUSHED IT!)

Rate yourself 1-5 on your leadership challenge this week

1   2   3   4   5

Rate 1-5 how well do you think you performed this week

1   2   3   4   5

Rate 1-5 how often you feel like you were consistent with your reps this week

1   2   3   4   5

Subject: You Need a Little Pie

Humble PIE, probably not the pie you were thinking. You have probably heard the saying before, maybe you need a piece of humble pie. I can guarantee that is not a pie you will see at your Thanksgiving table this year.

However, should it be? Faith and I hosted a Friendsgiving last night. There were tons of friends, lots of food, and laughs. You know what there wasn't? Pride.

Everyone came together and brought different items and we shared. We sat and talked, at one point and it felt like there were nine different conversations going on with only six of us there. When I took a second to look around, everyone had a true, genuine interest in each other's conversations.

Another cool thing I saw was compromise. See, one of the couples are huge UGA fans. The football game came on at 7:30. About the time dinner finished and games were about to start, what happened really without a beat the TV went on mute. We all gathered around the living room and played games together while the game was on.

It wasn't about one or the other couple's interests; it was about sharing and compromise.

"Okay, great Heath, I'm glad you had fun and all but what does your Friendsgiving have to do with humble pie?"

I have talked a lot in the past about being humble as a leader. However, I never really saw humility take place in a large group. Maybe it's just the holidays and I am getting all mushy.

Last night, I was able to see C.S. Lewis' quote come to life, "Humility is not thinking less of yourself, it's thinking of yourself less." To actually watch that take place was pretty awesome.

To apply action behind that quote, you must have the play button pressed on those two traits I mentioned earlier.

Sharing and compromise are two selfless acts. That speaks to someone's character and, in the business world, confidence.

Let me explain.

A lot of times as leaders we find little secrets of the trade here and there. Most times, if you are like the young and hungry business Heath, you wouldn't tell anyone. You thought you had cracked the code on leads or sales or something of that nature. Looking back now, how foolish. I didn't understand the power of sharing. See, I thought it was all about the hustle and grind. I could have worked smarter if I would have had a little humility. When I started to meet other business leaders and talk with them, that's when I started to see the power of sharing. There are so many great minds out there to be selfish and not share. I started to learn so much! I used to only train two clients in their homes ever in my eighteen years in the fitness industry. One, he owned restaurants and a consulting company and now a distillery. The other was one of the top female financial advisors for a large firm. I can't tell you the gratitude I owe these two individuals. They shared and taught me so much. When I opened the business at age twenty-five, I was learning at the school of hard knocks. Their shared wealth of knowledge helped me see that if I opened my network and started to share in my circle what could happen.

I also know this is scary to do in a corporate environment, where there is always that one person who takes your concept or idea and gets ahead on everyone else's sharing. That's okay. Trust me, they will have a hard lesson to learn at some point in their career.

How can sharing help you? As a leader, you need to share ideas and thoughts. Make sure whatever you are sharing, it's at the appropriate time to share. Meaning you have thought things through and are just looking for a little insight or confirmation. Share ideas that have worked for you! We did an exercise in our managers' meeting. I had you write down a problem you were struggling with. Then you passed to the person on your right and they had thirty seconds to share their idea. By the time we were done, you had eight different ideas, all shared by managers in your region.

Sharing will also help you get buy-in. I was sitting in a studio last week talking to two of the front desk girls and I shared an idea I had for a reward program; wanted to see if it got them excited or not.

You know what actually happened? They were more excited that I'd found value in sharing an idea with them than the actual reward program. The manager called and told me how excited they were; that I sat down and shared some ideas. Sharing shows I trust you with my car or my thoughts. Trust is the gateway to buy-in.

Secondly, you have to be able to compromise. I don't mean rollover and die. The compromise I am talking about is when both parties can put self aside and see the bigger picture of how X could affect the outcome. See, at our Friendsgiving, if we didn't compromise, there would have probably been a division of threes; three groups of people all doing something different.

Not when you can put *self* aside and compromise though, it's an exciting polar opposite from *self*. In the leadership world of compromise, I believe it comes down to push and pull.

How hard and where to push before you step in and help pull. If we have a goal of phone calls for the day, great, but what if we aren't booking appointments? You know your team doesn't enjoy making those calls. Is there a compromise? Maybe say thirty calls or three booked appointments, whichever comes first. Or how about you step in and say, "Tell you what, if you hit your revenue goal by X time on your shift, I'll pick up ten of your calls."

Find areas you can comprise with your team, but you have to remember you are still the leader. Don't become a pushover.

With everything we do, there is balance. I like ice cream but not every night. So make sure there is a good balance, as well as frequency. Be careful how often you compromise. Little doses go a long way. This is not the game show *Let's Make a Deal*. There is still work to be done. Just know where and when you can compromise!

I wanted to share how I visually saw humility take place and the two actions that prompted it.

What can you share this week with your team? Maybe even sharing in their responsibilities at work. Let them see you sharing the load. Sharing isn't just vocal; it's also physical.

What areas can you compromise in that could have positive impacts in your studios' moral and metrics?

Have a great week, everyone!

Subject: CPR Report

Free Space to write down key takeaways or answers to any questions found in this week's email:

_____

_____

_____

_____

Questions

Answer any challenging questions the email posed to you:

_____

_____

_____

_____

Challenge

What was the leadership challenge that spoke to you this week?

_____

_____

_____

_____

Perform

How do you plan to perform the challenges this week?

_____

_____

_____

_____

Repetitions

What do you need to do to remind yourself to get your reps in this week?

_____

_____

_____

_____

CPR Progress Report

(1 Needed Major Improvement - 5 CRUSHED IT!)

Rate yourself 1-5 on your leadership challenge this week

1   2   3   4   5

Rate 1-5 how well do you think you performed this week

1   2   3   4   5

Rate 1-5 how often you feel like you were consistent with your reps this week

1   2   3   4   5

Subject: Are You Plugged In?

One of my all-time favorite Christmas movies is the classic, "National Lampoon's Christmas Vacation." I believe it's so relatable to so many people. There is at least one scene in that movie everyone can relate with.

Mine is when he is hanging the lights; every part, from when he is on the ladder to untangling the lights, trying to find the right plugs and switches to turn them on. Such a classic scene.

Since we are in the year 2020 and there is nothing traditional about this year, Faith and I have already started putting up our Christmas trees. Just for a point of reference, it's November 16th. I can't tell you a time we have even had Christmas decorations out before Black Friday.

I actually really enjoyed helping setting up and decorating the trees. We put on some Hallmark movies and poured a glass of wine. Then we had fun decorating our four, possibly this year five trees. What can I say? We love Christmas.

Now when you start talking about decorating the outside of the house. This is where things get a little stressful for me, hanging the lights.

Two of the most frustrating things about hanging the lights are the heights and the bulbs.

Thinking about what to write this week, those two frustrations kept poking at me. I want to take a second and unpack each of this and help understand how to turn those frustrations into fulfillment.

Let's first take a look at heights. Man, this is a fear of mine for sure. I am not a huge fan of heights. When Faith and I cruise, I refuse to get a balcony room. I just can't do the heights. There is a part of me that is strangely curious; the other louder part is terrified. I just try to avoid heights as much as possible. I am talking about heights in the physical sense. I have never been afraid of the ladder of progress. There is one thing I learned through from putting up those Christmas lights, and climbing my behind on top of my house roofline, to outline our window at the peak of our roof with lights and stick a wreath on it.

It's not the height that's scary; it's the instability of the ladder. The climb is scary when the ladder is creaking and cracking. It's swaying side to side, or it slips a little bit on the shingles.

But when you have someone holding the ladder at the bottom, the whole climb changes. You see, I think as leaders we rarely finish the climb. Because when you look down it's empty; there is no one holding you steady. That sets us into a state of paralysis and we never complete the climb. Or we climb down and find a new shiny ladder that isn't so tall.

I have learned over the last couple of years being a leader isn't about being the first to the top of that "corporate ladder"; it's actually about holding it for others. The heights are only scary when you are on the journey alone. But when you bring a team with you and you can hold the ladder for each other, that height is a little less intimidating. I will also tell you the amount of trust you can build with a team when they see you holding it for them instead of stepping on their heads to get over them. You will never be able to find another way to build that level of trust.

Whose ladder have you held recently? Do you feel like everyone on your team is stuck on a different rung on their ladder? Take some time this week and help a few of your team members advance on their ladders.

Next are the bulbs. I look at the bulbs, like our business Key Performance Indicators. When they are all in check and running in sync, they are all lit up and it's bright.

But when you have that one bulb, that one bulb goes out, it can shut down an entire string of lights. That one metric is off and the cascade effect goes into play.

The good news is there is a simple way to prevent the infuriating case of *Guess which bulb is bad.*

You can simply plug them in before you start to hang them. You take a second before your day begins and plug into your metrics; take a look at some KPI's that could potentially be dimming.

You know the ones; the ones that you just don't have a good answer for right now.

Have you taken a second to ask your team their opinions? Sometimes those who are on the ground can see the problem with the lights faster than the one hanging them. Their vantage point is different.

If a bulb does go out, big deal. It's an easy fix, you just have to revisit it and plug in a new fresh idea or strategy.

Which leads me to my question: Which bulb is currently either out or dimming on your strand? Do you have a replacement ready? Have you asked your team for help?

While these two things may be very frustrating about hanging Christmas lights, I can promise you: The outcome is worth the obstacles, only if you properly know how to navigate through them.

Subject: **CPR Report**

Free Space to write down key takeaways or answers to any questions found in this week's email:

_____

_____

_____

_____

Questions

Answer any challenging questions the email posed to you:

_____

_____

_____

_____

Challenge

What was the leadership challenge that spoke to you this week?

_____

_____

_____

_____

Perform

How do you plan to perform the challenges this week?

_____

_____

_____

_____

Repetitions

What do you need to do to remind yourself to get your reps
in this week?

_____

_____

_____

_____

CPR Progress Report

(1 Needed Major Improvement - 5 CRUSHED IT!)

Rate yourself 1-5 on your leadership challenge this week

1   2   3   4   5

Rate 1-5 how well do you think you performed this week

1   2   3   4   5

Rate 1-5 how often you feel like you were consistent with
your reps this week

1   2   3   4   5

Subject: Baking for Success

When I was younger, the day after Thanksgiving, my mom would start baking cookies like she was a Keebler elf. My dad is a pastor, and every year we would host an open house for Christmas at our house.

I can remember helping my mom bake every kind of cookie possible, along with other sweet treats. We would sit down on Friday nights and watch T.G.I.F. and decorate cookies for hours.

We used to come home from school and there would be flour on all the counters. On the counters, you'd see mixing bowls, wooden spoons, packs of half-used butter. Then, there'd be fresh cookie dough in the fridge.

The baking ingredients are well thought out. Consideration is given to the proper flavor profiles and the exact amounts so one doesn't overpower the other. We all worked in harmony together to create the proper consistency for proper baking.

People who cook know it's a little easier to eyeball the ingredients. When comparing cooking with baking, you can't eyeball baking. You have to have the exact amount of sugar, butter, baking soda, flour, eggs, and vanilla extract.

I think what makes baking fun is the ingredients themselves. For the most part, there are about four basic ingredients when baking cookies. You have flour, sugar, shortening, and liquids. Sounds simple right? Well, if you want a basic cookie, yes! However, my mom was not in the cookie game for basic.

For the purpose of this email, we are going to stick to basic ingredients. I was thinking about basic ingredients that go into making a leader and an easy way to remember. So whether you are sitting in your office or you are stuck in traffic on your way to a meeting, maybe you are baking cookies.

You can always remember B.A.K.E.

Boldness is our first ingredient of leadership. There is a great quote I saw. I'm not sure who to give the credit to, "Be bold to do what the ordinary fear." Just like baked goods have to be bold in flavor, leaders need to be bold not brash! I love thinking about innovative historical leaders. They had no choice other than to be bold. They also stepped out of the comfort zone and took risks the ordinary wouldn't.

The first couple who come to my mind, Walt Disney and Henry Ford. How many times do you think people around these two told them they were crazy? How many times do you think others said, "*That will never work?*" That's because ordinary people fear innovation; they like that their cars only went ten mph. Not Henry.

Do you think they listened? Of course not! Because they were bold and believed. Now don't mistake they were also very calculated. They took bold stands for what they believed in. As a leader, you must be bold in your beliefs.

Being bold is a risk. If you have ever baked and want big, bold flavor, you are taking a risk. Don't be afraid of being bold. We will always need leaders who question what is possible; ones who come to the table with solutions to existing problems.

Adaptability is the second leadership ingredient. When baking, your ingredients become adaptable. They are forced to change and adapt to the changing environment around them. In the world of work, you hear adaptability a lot; and for good reason. The world of work has never changed as fast as it has this year with the global pandemic. Businesses had to pivot and make changes daily to survive. Workers had to be able to learn how to work from home as well as become teachers.

As a leader, you have never known adaptability like you do now in 2020. There were probably a lot of leaders who struggled and maybe still are because they aren't learning the new skills required in their new environments.

Being adaptable as a leader is having a plan, while also knowing what flexibility you have inside that plan; like dough can be molded and formed because of the state it's in. But once you put it in the oven and it begins to bake, there is a point of no longer being adaptable, and when pressure is applied, the cookie will crumble.

As a leader, never get to the baked cookie stage in your ability to be adaptable.

Key is our next ingredient of leadership. Like flour, this is the structure for cookies; it kind of binds all ingredients together. Everyone has a key to their leadership structure. This is what makes you special as a leader. There is always an intangible key ingredient all leaders naturally have. It's like all good bakers have a special key ingredient that makes their recipes stand out in a crowd.

I want you to take a second and think about what your key ingredient is. Then thank God for it! Because it's yours; you were given it on purpose.

The next question is *How often do you use it?* If I had a special key ingredient for a cookie, I would always use it:

whether I was cooking it for myself, my friends, or entering into a contest.

Don't waste your key ingredient; it's unique to you.

Engagement is our final ingredient. Just like a baker is engaged in their cookies through the entire process, a leader must be engaged with his/her team and business. A disengaged baker will have burned cookies and eggshells in his/her dough. As a leader, you must stay engaged with your people, the process, and your product.

Are you engaged with your team?

Have you preheated your team? You need to set the proper expectations for them. Then follow up on them.

Have you checked on their temperature? Is your team too done because you left them in the heat too long? You pushed a little too hard and left them in the oven too long.

Don't become a disengaged leader who cooks their people too long.

This week, I am going to offer you three challenges:

If you don't know what your key ingredient to your leadership is, find out! Ask around; I am sure someone has seen it.

What new skill do you need to learn in the next thirty days to be a little more flexible and adaptable? Then find the answers.

Write down the last time you were bold. What big risk did you take and how did you feel afterward?

Subject: CPR Report

Free Space to write down key takeaways or answers to any questions found in this week's email:

_____

_____

_____

_____

Questions

Answer any challenging questions the email posed to you:

_____

_____

_____

_____

Challenge

What was the leadership challenge that spoke to you this week?

_____

_____

_____

_____

Perform

How do you plan to perform the challenges this week?

_____

_____

_____

_____

Repetitions

What do you need to do to remind yourself to get your reps
in this week?

_____

_____

_____

_____

CPR Progress Report

(1 Needed Major Improvement - 5 CRUSHED IT!)

Rate yourself 1-5 on your leadership challenge this week

1   2   3   4   5

Rate 1-5 how well do you think you performed this week

1   2   3   4   5

Rate 1-5 how often you feel like you were consistent with
your reps this week

1   2   3   4   5

Subject: Decorating Your Leadership

Over the years, Faith and I have slowly added additional Christmas trees here and there. Now we have four trees; all are themed and in different places in the house.

We have our dining room tree; this one is more of a wine-themed tree. Then we can travel over to my office for the rustic woods and metal tree. The winter wonderland tree can be found in the corner of our bedroom. Lastly, you can't help when you walk into our house but see the main tree. This is the tallest, fullest, and most decorated tree in the house.

As I have said before, in the year 2020, we started to decorate early; except for the main tree, we waited till the day after Thanksgiving to put this one up. While decorating our trees this year, I started thinking about the word *decorate*. What does it mean? How does it apply to leadership?

Lights usually go on first when decorating your tree. The lights are there to give your tree personality. There are so many different kinds of light options for your tree. Each leader is going to bring their individual personality to their leadership style. This is where I see too many people trying to replicate what they can't consistently reproduce. If you try to talk, act, and lead like someone else, you will ultimately fail. It's just not in your DNA. You have a God-given personality. You can change things that influence you, like choosing to be more positive and other small habit changes like that. But you have a unique personality like lights on a tree. Let's take a look at three different types:

- Multi-Colored Lights: These are the more eccentric personality leaders. They are usually a little more unconventional and have slightly different views. They are always willing to try something new.

- Twinkling Lights: These are your enthusiastic personality leaders. They are full of life and energy, typically going be your more natural motivators. When you are excited, your team is excited.

- Solid White Lights: These are your reliable personality leaders. They typically stick to tried and true methods. Their teams know what to expect from them. You love consistency and control.

Ribbon sets the vision and theme for your tree. The minute you change the ribbon color, size, any variant at all, you change the whole landscape of the tree. Just like with every great leader, you need clear vision and a theme. This will lay the foundation for decorating the rest of your tree. With a clear vision and theme to your leadership, you are able to build from there. Without the leader being clear on their vision, your tree will look cluttered and unorganized. People may be confused by what the theme is if your vision is off.

John Maxwell says, "Clarity of vision creates clarity of priorities." When you have a clear vision, anyone looking on can see the theme of your leadership.

When was the last time you visited your vision as a leader, company, husband? Is your vision confusing to others? Take a moment and write down your company's vision. Then write down your vision as a leader. Lastly, write down a vision for your studio. Do you think your team can see clarity in the vision, or is that why they lack clarity of priority?

Special Ornaments: Like in the military, a decorated leader will have multiple medals, service ribbons, specific badges, and colored bars. These are an outward display that highlights the service members' careers, as well as their rank. I am sure with each of those accomplishments there is a memory and experience behind each one of them.

This is what came to mind when decorating our main tree. There are those special ornaments. They are the memories, stories, and accomplishments you have gathered over the years.

Like any leader, you will gather special ornaments to decorate your leadership tree. Show these off proudly, and make sure you never forget how and where you got that special ornament from. These are those moments that make up the leader you are currently.

Think about your special leadership ornaments. Which ones would you put front and center on your leadership tree? Which one do you feel makes your team feel confident in you as a leader? Which accomplishment has the best story?

Standard Solid Color Ornaments: These are the gap fillers. In every leadership tree, there are going to be bare spots that stand out from any angle. These are the areas you haven't filled in yet with a special ornament yet. Maybe you haven't grown in that area of your leadership yet, and it's still bare there. The good news about the solid ornaments is they show you opportunity.

The question is, are you happy just filling the gaps with a solid color? Or is it time to grab a book, listen to a podcast, take some time, and create a memory with your team as a leader, maybe it's time to step out of your comfort zone and achieve something new with greater results.

Write down three gaps in your leadership you would like to fill. Maybe it's time management. How about keeping your team accountable, achieving what you may think is a "crazy" goal? Write those down. Then set a date you want to complete these by. This time next year, your tree will have a little less bare spots and three more unique ornaments.

The tree topper is usually the last item you put on the tree. In most movies, it's usually saved for the dad, who is always out of town when the tree is being decorated. The tree topper is the pinnacle of your tree.

On your leadership tree, the tree topper is your proudest accomplishment as a leader. Accomplishments are something you can be proud of. Just be careful when you put your accomplishments on display keep them in perspective.

Like most of us have probably been asked in an interview, what is your biggest accomplishment as a leader?

When you decorate your leadership tree, don't just look at the beauty look at the bald spots. Look for those areas that you can beautify.

Subject: CPR Report

Free Space to write down key takeaways or answers to any questions found in this week's email:

_____

_____

_____

_____

Questions

Answer any challenging questions the email posed to you:

_____

_____

_____

_____

Challenge

What was the leadership challenge that spoke to you this week?

_____

_____

_____

_____

Perform

How do you plan to perform the challenges this week?

_____

_____

_____

_____

Repetitions

What do you need to do to remind yourself to get your reps in this week?

_____

_____

_____

_____

CPR Progress Report

(1 Needed Major Improvement - 5 CRUSHED IT!)

Rate yourself 1-5 on your leadership challenge this week

1   2   3   4   5

Rate 1-5 how well do you think you performed this week

1   2   3   4   5

Rate 1-5 how often you feel like you were consistent with your reps this week

1   2   3   4   5

Subject: That's a WRAP

Okay, so this is the email before the email. You are either confused or overwhelmed after that opening statement.

Let me explain. Every Christmas time, the leadership emails are tied into some of the Christmas movie favorites. This year, however, I have gone in a different direction with the December emails.

So I decided to give you a bonus email today. You may not be as excited as I am about it. I promise if you take the time to break them down and digest them, you will be thankful you did.

This time every year, people go out and buy gifts they think others will like. It's so funny most of the time these gifts aren't even needed; they are wanted. Have you ever been sitting there looking at a possible gift and thinking, *Do you think they want this or will like this?*

So you buy this gift you think they will like. You get it home and are proud of your purchase. Then comes the wrapping of that gift. You cover up this gift you are so proud of.

I think this is funny. I was never a big gift wrapper until I married Faith. I was more of the gift bag or plain wrapping paper kind of gift wrapper.

Not with Faith! We now have shiny wrapping paper with glitter, bows, ribbons, and stickers. These gifts are beautifully wrapped. You remember the gifts that we think others will like; the gifts we were proud and excited to purchase.

As we were WRAPPING gifts last night, I started asking myself, *Why do we cover up these gifts? Is it because we try and make the gift look more appealing than it actually is? Are we a little insecure that they may not actually like the gift, so we try and WRAP in pretty paper to distract? Are you trying to make your gift look bigger than it actually is by putting it in a bigger box and then WRAP it?*

I feel like sometimes young and mature leaders try and WRAP up four leadership characteristics. I would encourage you to think about these four characteristics below. Then ask yourself, *Am I wrapping any of these up for the reasons listed below, or maybe another reason?* These four are the gifts your team needs, not just wants. And as a leader, if they are wrapped up, your team and others are receiving coal.

Wisdom. Leaders wrap up their wisdom to distract. They don't wrap it because they don't want to share it. They wrap it up because they want to distract from the fact they don't know it. The problem with wrapping the gift of wisdom is your team actually needs this from their leader! If you are not taking the steps to improve your wisdom as a leader and business person, your team will become depleted of growth and you will never be able to retain a team. Wisdom is essential for a healthy studio, and a growing team!

Respect. Leaders sometimes wrap up their respect because it's phony. They don't actually respect others they work with, or their direct reports. They do this because they think this phony respect will allow them to stay in good standing with those they work with and work for. Phony respect is easy to detect. No matter how many bows and ribbons you have on this package, phony respect will always be exposed. Your team wants to respect their leadership; if they don't feel that respect back, you will never earn theirs. You don't always have to like the decisions that are made. But you have to be able to respect the one making them.

Attitude. Leaders wrap up their attitudes because they don't have control. Attitude is all about choice. You choose to be positive or negative. I worked at GNC in college. My first day on the job, the manager Ed told me, "I don't care what's happening outside of work. When you cross the threshold of the store, you represent health and wellness." What that meant to me is I have to *choose* how I approach work. You have to control your attitude at all times. If you don't wake up and choose to control your attitude, you are a loose cannon! Your team deserves a leader that can control their attitude.

Passion. Leaders wrap up passion to try and replicate it. Too many times, I see others in leadership positions who aren't actually passionate about the position, they are passionate about the title. The thing about passion is you can't replicate it. You will never be able to perform any job or position well if you aren't truly passionate. I saw true passion this past weekend. Passion is selfless: it's caring; it requires action; it doesn't require an acknowledgment. There is no way you can replicate those above. Your team craves a passionate leader. Become one; don't try and replicate one.

Start to unwrap these gifts your team's needs!

bject: **CPR Report**

Free Space to write down key takeaways or answers to any questions found in this week's email:

_____

_____

_____

_____

Questions

Answer any challenging questions the email posed to you:

_____

_____

_____

_____

Challenge

What was the leadership challenge that spoke to you this week?

_____

_____

_____

_____

Perform

How do you plan to perform the challenges this week?

_____

_____

_____

_____

Repetitions

What do you need to do to remind yourself to get your reps in this week?

_____

_____

_____

_____

CPR Progress Report

(1 Needed Major Improvement - 5 CRUSHED IT!)

Rate yourself 1-5 on your leadership challenge this week

1   2   3   4   5

Rate 1-5 how well do you think you performed this week

1   2   3   4   5

Rate 1-5 how often you feel like you were consistent with your reps this week

1   2   3   4   5

If you are anything like me, you have probably watched "Home Alone" a half dozen times between Thanksgiving and Christmas.

Every year, I can't help but laugh out loud at Harry and Marv's discomfort and misfortune. I don't believe there was anyone else who could have played those roles better.

I also find little hidden business secrets sprinkled throughout the movie. You're saying, *"Heath, I have seen that movie and it never taught me a single thing about business."*

That's okay! You just enjoy the movie. Let me share the lessons.

What I want to do is walk you through the *defend your studio blueprint*. This way, no matter when Harry and Marv show up in your neighborhood, you can stand up and say, *"This is my studio and I have to defend it!"*

Any good blueprint starts with a sketch of the floor plan. This is a bird's eye view of the layout. You need to be able to see it from 30,000 feet. Once on ground level, you have walls in your way and other barricades that will prevent you from the successful construction of the vantage point.

If you remember, in the movie, Kevin pulls out a blueprint of his house, each room and entry point accounted for. Each one has been carefully outlined with a booby-trap needed to either prevent or slow down entry.

I look at Kevin's blueprint as calculated business moves, all well throughout and executed to perfection. I feel like a lot of times we are only focused on the front door and the two windows beside it. How many points of entry/exit do you have mapped out daily/weekly/monthly? Do you have a plan for each?

Think about the rooms in his house as the different KPIs we talk about. Then attach a booby-trap to that KPI. What's going to stop that metric from negatively impacting your studio? If you wanted a visual, think about the scoreboard I have shown you all. This is your blueprint. It offers clarity for calculated moves.

Why weren't Harry and Marv successful at outsmarting a ten-year-old? They weren't calculated in their moves. They underestimated the preparedness of young Kevin. They were also at a disadvantage. Kevin had all the tools and insight he needed to set those booby-traps. Just like with each of you, you all have the advantage. You have resources and support to set those business booby-traps.

The Sticky Bandits were also not successful because they became frustrated and desperate. You will never win when those two emotions come into the frame. When you are frustrated, you don't tend to think clearly and only react out of anger, which can lead to oversight of details. Desperate attitudes lead to stupid decisions; and that becomes, "What do you have to lose actions."

Now flip the script. What if Kevin would have been the frustrated and desperate one? He wasn't bigger, stronger, or faster than Harry and Marv. He would have probably been hanging by his sweater, missing all his fingers and the story then become a horror movie.

However, that's not the case. He stayed calm and calculated. Most importantly, he stuck to his plan and worked it. He didn't stray from what he planned. He dedicated himself to that plan and worked it.

Let's make a blueprint for success this week. How many booby-traps can you set and stay dedicated to working your plan?

Subject: **CPR Report**

Free Space to write down key takeaways or answers to any questions found in this week's email:

_____

_____

_____

_____

Questions

Answer any challenging questions the email posed to you:

_____

_____

_____

_____

Challenge

What was the leadership challenge that spoke to you this week?

_____

_____

_____

_____

Perform

How do you plan to perform the challenges this week?

_____

_____

_____

_____

Repetitions

What do you need to do to remind yourself to get your reps in this week?

_____

_____

_____

_____

CPR Progress Report

(1 Needed Major Improvement - 5 CRUSHED IT!)

Rate yourself 1-5 on your leadership challenge this week

1   2   3   4   5

Rate 1-5 how well do you think you performed this week

1   2   3   4   5

Rate 1-5 how often you feel like you were consistent with your reps this week

1   2   3   4   5

Are you finished?

Yes, finished with this book. What you are not finished with is giving your team what they deserve: a commitment to continued growth as their leader.

I had a conversation the other day with an assistant manager at one of our locations. He asked me, "Heath, how do you show up every day and bring the level of energy and positivity that you do?" My response was, "Do you know what my biggest fear is?" He looked at me and I could tell he was completely thrown off guard by my response to his question with a question.

He then asked, "What's your biggest fear?" I smiled and thanked him for asking. "My biggest fear is letting each of you down." I then continued, "I don't have time to be upset or negative because it doesn't help me with my ultimate purpose of impacting people in a positive way. Every day, I choose to be full of life. I choose to have a positive attitude. More importantly, I give 150 percent with every interaction and conversation I have. Whether it be on the Wednesday sales call, in manager meetings, in the emails I write, speaking at a convention, or even this conversation right here. At the end of the day, when that voice starts to creep in my head and tells me I didn't do enough or I could have done better, I can cut it off quickly knowing that I gave everything I had with every interaction I had." He looked at me and smiled. He then said, "Sometimes I have that voice too; it usually defeats me." I smiled back and told him, "Now you know how to defeat it. You choose to defeat it with giving all that you have in every situation and interaction."

I hope that after completing all fifty-two weekly lessons, you have all the tools to defeat that voice in your head.

Over the course of this book, you have been challenged. Not just challenged personally, but you have been encouraged to pass those challenges onto those you support and serve. I hope you received these challenges as a way to give yourself and your team a better viewpoint of circumstances and situations. I love what Steven Furtick says about challenges: "The challenge in front of you is an indication of the power within you." Challenges are like video game levels. Once you have learned the challenges in level one, you are able to complete it and move to the next level. Level two isn't designed to be easier. But now with the right tools and resources, you are better equipped for that challenge.

You have also been asked to perform. If you have used the CPR reports after each email, you will see there was an opportunity to perform an exercise in self-evaluation and self-reflection, which is a valuable lesson in itself. The great John Wooden said, "Without proper self-evaluation, failure is inevitable."

You may have had to perform some tough evaluations of yourself, your business, and your staff. What I can promise is by performing those exercises honestly, you are creating a better environment for everyone.

Lastly, you have been empowered to take repetitions in performing these new challenges. I only thought it was appropriate to allow Zig Ziglar to drop the mic with his quote about repetitions. He says, "Repetition is the Mother of learning, the Father of action, which makes it the architect of accomplishment." When I was training clients for all those years, I could have provided the proper challenge, showed how to perform. But, without the action of repetition, no change would have happened. Repetitions are hard and will create fatigue. That's good; it means it's working. Just know this, there will be a time when that ten-pound weight is no longer causing fatigue. This means you have created the muscle necessary to accomplish that task. It's time to grab fifteen pounds.

Your leadership muscles will grow and adapt to the challenges. When that happens, apply some leadership CPR compressions to pump liveliness into your bloodstream. This way when that voice starts to creep into your head and tries to tell you, "They deserve better," you can respond, "They don't deserve better; they got my best."

Bibliography

Andrew, Andy. 2009. The Noticer. Gale.

Briggs, Saga. 2017. "The Science of Attention: How to Capture and Hold the Attention of Easily Distracted Students | InformED." InformED. April 29, 2017. https://www.opencolleges.edu.au/informed/features/30-tricks-for-capturing-students-attention/.

"C. S. Lewis Quote: 'True Humility Is Not Thinking Less of Yourself; It Is Thinking of Yourself Less.'" n.d. Quotefancy.com. Accessed March 11, 2021. https://quotefancy.com/quote/6930/C-S-Lewis-True-humility-is-not-thinking-less-of-yourself-it-is-thinking-of-yourself-less.

"Clarity of Vision Creates Clarity of Priorities. John C. Maxwell." 2018. The Mindset Journey. June 14, 2018. https://www.themindsetjourney.com/motivational-quotes/clarity-of-vision-creates-clarity-of-priorities-john-c-maxwell/.

"Commitment, N." n.d. Oxford English Dictionary. Oxford University Press. Accessed March 11, 2021. https://www.oed.com/view/Entry/37161?redirectedFrom=Commitment+#eid.

eligenza. 2015. "'The Grass Is Greener Where You Water It.' - Monday Mantra." Coming up Roses. November 2, 2015. https://cominguprosestheblog.com/the-grass-is-green-where-you-water-it/.

Furtick, Steven. 2020. "Https://Twitter.com/Stevenfurtick/Status/1279195731434385408." Twitter. July 23, 2020. https://twitter.com/stevenfurtick/status/1279195731434385408.

"Inspire, V." n.d. Oxford English Dictionary. Oxford University Press. Accessed March 11, 2021. https://www.oed.com/view/Entry/96990?redirectedFrom=Inspire+#eid.

"John C. Maxwell Quote: 'Momentum Solves 80% of Your Problems.'" n.d. Quotefancy.com. Accessed March 11, 2021. https://quotefancy.com/quote/841457/John-C-Maxwell-Momentum-solves-80-of-your-problems.

"John Wooden Quote." n.d. A-Z Quotes. Accessed March 11, 2021. https://www.azquotes.com/quote/1217466.

"John Wooden Quote: 'It's the Little Details That Are Vital. Little Things Make Big Things Happen.'" n.d. Quotefancy.com. Accessed March 11, 2021. https://quotefancy.com/quote/53482/John-Wooden-It-s-the-little-details-that-are-vital-Little-things-make-big-things-happen.

"John Wooden Quote: 'without Proper Self-Evaluation, Failure Is Inevitable.'" n.d. Quotefancy.com. https://quotefancy.com/quote/845172/John-Wooden-Without-proper-self-evaluation-failure-is-inevitable.

Li, Lori. 2020. "17 Surprising Statistics about Employee Retention." TINYpulse. September 8, 2020. https://www.tinypulse.com/blog/17-surprising-statistics-about-employee-retention.

"Lou Holtz Quote: 'It's Not the Load That Breaks You Down, It's the Way You Carry It.'" n.d. Quotefancy.com. Accessed March 11, 2021. https://quotefancy.com/quote/951/Lou-Holtz-It-s-not-the-load-that-breaks-you-down-it-s-the-way-you-carry-it.

Mcchesney, Chris, Sean Covey, and Jim Huling. 2016. The 4 Disciplines of Execution : Achieving Your Wildly Important Goals. New York: Free Press.

"Napoleon Quote: 'a Leader Is a Dealer in Hope.'"
n.d. Quotefancy.com. Accessed March 11,
2021. https://quotefancy.com/quote/23829/
Napoleon-A-leader-is-a-dealer-in-hope.

Pesce, Nicole Lyn. 2013. "It's Not Easy to Land a Job as
a Balloon Handler in the Macy's Thanksgiving Day
Parade." Nydailynews.com. November 10, 2013. https://
www.nydailynews.com/life-style/not-easy-landing-job-
balloon-handler-macy-parade-article-1.1510167.

Ranjan, Hagel III, J.S.B, and Byler. 2014. "Passion at Work:
Cultivating Worker Passion as a Cornerstone of Talent
Development | Deloitte Insights." Www2.Deloitte.
com. October 7, 2014. https://www2.deloitte.com/us/
en/insights/topics/talent/worker-passion-employee-
behavior.html.

"SEAL Ethos." 2021. Www.nsw.navy.mil. March 10, 2021.
https://www.nsw.navy.mil/NSW/SEAL-Ethos/.

"Sometimes the Grass Is Greener on the Other Side
Because It's Fake. | Wise Quotes, Motivational
Quotes for Life, Words Quotes." n.d. Pinterest.
Accessed March 12, 2021. https://www.pinterest.com/
pin/291537775877897304/.

"Stephen R. Covey Quote: 'the Key Is Not to Prioritize
What's on Your Schedule, but to Schedule Your
Priorities.'" n.d. Quotefancy.com. Accessed March 11,
2021. https://quotefancy.com/quote/757966/Stephen-
R-Covey-The-key-is-not-to-prioritize-what-s-on-your-
schedule-but-to-schedule-your.

"Stephen R. Covey Quote: 'What You Do Has Far Greater
Impact than What You Say.'" n.d. Quotefancy.com.
Accessed March 11, 2021. https://quotefancy.com/
quote/909263/Stephen-R-Covey-What-you-do-has-far-
greater-impact-than-what-you-say.

"Tactical, Adj." n.d. Oxford English Dictionary. Oxford University Press. Accessed March 11, 2021. https://www.oed.com/view/Entry/196964?redirectedFrom=tactical#eid.

Wikipedia Contributors. 2019. "Ethos." Wikipedia. Wikimedia Foundation. April 23, 2019. https://en.wikipedia.org/wiki/Ethos.

"Zig Ziglar Quote: 'Repetition Is the Mother of Learning, the Father of Action, Which Makes It the Architect of Accomplishment.'" n.d. Quotefancy.com. Accessed March 11, 2021. https://quotefancy.com/quote/943341/Zig-Ziglar-Repetition-is-the-mother-of-learning-the-father-of-action-which-makes-it-the.

CPSIA information can be obtained
at www.ICGtesting.com
Printed in the USA
BVHW080826240421
605735BV00003B/219

9 781662 810480